About the Author

Theresa Cheung was born into a family of psychics and spiritualists. Since gaining a masters degree from King's College, Cambridge, she has been involved in the serious study of the paranormal for over 25 years and has been a student of the College of Psychic Studies in London. She is the author of a variety of books, including the international bestseller *The Element Encyclopedia of 20,000 Dreams* as well as *The Element Encyclopedia of the Psychic World, The Element Encyclopedia of Birthdays* and *Working with Your Sixth Sense.* Her books have been translated into 20 different languages and her writing has also featured in *It's Fate, Spirit and Destiny* and *Prediction* magazines. She has also worked on books for Derek Acorah, Yvette Fielding and Tony Stockwell.

Theresa believes both this book and her first angel book *An Angel Called My Name* were born in answer to her own questions and as a gift to her and others. She has a great interest in angels, spirit guides, dreams and visions of the afterlife and feels that the angels are directing her writing and her life. She has also had several angel experiences herself, some of which she shares here.

D0608766

If you have had an angel experience and wish to share it with Theresa she would love to hear from you. Please contact her care of HarperElement, Editorial Department, 77–85 Fulham Palace Road, London W6 8JB, or email any inspiring and uplifting stories direct to her at angeltalk710@aol.com.

An Angel
on my shoulder

An Angel on my shoulder

Inspiring true stories from the other side

Theresa Cheung

HarperElement
An Imprint of HarperCollins*Publishers*
77–85 Fulham Palace Road,
Hammersmith, London W6 8JB

www.harpercollins.co.uk

and *HarperElement* are trademarks of
HarperCollins*Publishers* Ltd

First published by HarperElement 2008

1 3 5 7 9 10 8 6 4 2

© Theresa Cheung 2008

A catalogue record of this book is
available from the British Library

ISBN 978-0-00-728880-9

Printed and bound in Great Britain by
Clays Ltd, St Ives plc

FSC is a non-profit international organisation established to promote the
responsible management of the world's forests. Products carrying the FSC
label are independently certified to assure consumers that they come
from forests that are managed to meet the social, economic and
ecological needs of present and future generations.

Find out more about HarperCollins and the environment at
www.harpercollins.co.uk/green

May you always have an angel on your shoulder.

Contents

Introduction: Why I Believe in Angels

There are two ways to live your life.
One is as though nothing is a miracle.
The other is as though everything is a miracle.

Albert Einstein

Yes, I believe in angels. I always have. I believe that there are angels in the afterlife and angels resting on my shoulder right here on Earth! I think that we tend to chalk a lot of things up to coincidence, lucky breaks, close calls or being in the right place at the right time, but if you have ever felt a magical, loving presence around you I believe this is the work of your guardian angel. I also believe that angels can speak through your intuition or your dreams or the spirits of loved ones who have passed to the other side. And sometimes they appear in the guise of other people or animals, consciously or unconsciously guided by those from a higher dimension.

First of all, I believe in angels because that is what I was taught to believe as a child. My mother was a psychic and my grandmother and great aunt were both clairvoyants, so angels have always been a part of my life. I have simply taken it for granted that they are always there to watch over me, guide me and comfort me and, when my time on Earth is up, to accompany me to the other world.

One of my mother's favourite sayings was: 'Wherever I go, I call on my guardian angel to be with me – to be above me, below me, beside me, in front of me, behind me and within me.' And angels were with her. One day – I must have been about seven at the time – she picked me up from school and told me we were going to drive out of town to visit a dear friend of hers in hospital. Her friend had suffered a stroke and, as I would discover a week later, had only days to live. We drove for about half an hour and then Mum must have taken a wrong turn or something because it soon became clear we were heading in the wrong direction. Although I was young, I sensed how important it was for Mum to see her friend that evening. It didn't help that it was midwinter and the weather was extremely bad, with thick fog refusing to budge. The roads were fairly quiet, but driving was still hazardous. Mum could barely see the markings on the road.

Suddenly the steering wheel jerked in Mum's hands and she lurched from the slow lane of a dual carriageway into the fast lane to overtake a car travelling ahead of us. As she overtook the car she came dangerously close to bumping into it and this uncharacteristically bad driving forced it to swerve. Understandably infuriated, the driver hooted his horn several times and, obviously still angry, proceeded to over (or is it under?) take us via the slow lane before cutting in front of us in the fast lane.

Unaware of just how hazardous Mum's erratic driving had been, I found it all wildly exciting. As we watched the car speed off and disappear in the fog ahead of us I asked Mum if she was going to play catch-up and follow that car. She shook her head and told me a voice was telling her to stay in the fast lane, but this didn't mean she had to drive really, really fast.

By now we were approaching a bridge. The fog was getting really thick. I looked out of the window and saw the hazy figures of two people frantically pushing a car from the slow lane to the side of the road. The stalled car was moving, but as we drove past it was still blocking much of the slow lane. If we had stayed in that lane we would almost certainly have slammed into it because the fog was so heavy and the car being pushed out of the road had no lights on. My mum slowed to a crawl as we passed by, with her emergency lights flashing to warn cars coming behind, and we watched the car being pushed off the road, relieved that it was no longer a threat to traffic in the slow lane.

We were just about to speed up again when there, shining in the headlights, my mum noticed a nearly concealed sign pointing us in the right direction to the hospital.

My mum later told me her guardian angel had driven her car that day and that very same angel had made sure she had found a sign to direct her to the hospital to see her friend one last time. She also told me that an angel had saved not just our lives as we headed to the hospital but the lives of the people in the stalled car and the life of the driver with road rage. If her guardian angel hadn't made her overtake the car ahead and made the driver angry, he would have stayed in the slow lane and crashed. She explained that angels can manifest in the most unusual and unexpected ways. I believed her.

Then there was the time, a year or so later, when we had hardly any food left in the house. All the earnings from Mum's psychic counselling service had recently been spent on repairing our leaky roof. We were used to living on very little but not this little, and for days we ate nothing but pasta, cheese and apples. It was all we could afford. At no point, though, was my mum distressed or anxious. She told us that we shouldn't worry because she had asked her guardian angel to make sure we would not starve. And she was right.

One afternoon there was a knock at the front door. When Mum opened it a young woman in a blue dress, yellow cardigan and brown sandals stood there smiling. This lovely woman told us that she was a close friend of Jean, our next-door neighbour. She said she hoped we would not be offended, but Jean had told her we could really use some supplies. Then she explained that she was moving house the next day and needed to clear out her kitchen cupboards, fridge and freezer. With open mouths and growling stomachs we stared at the bags of groceries lined up on the floor beside her. There were dozens of them, brimful of tins, packets, fruit, vegetables and other essentials. Our mouths stayed open as we watched her drive away in her little white Mini.

We ate well that night and for several nights after, and the grocery gift was enough to tide us through a really rough patch financially. A bit overwhelmed by this act of kindness from a stranger, Mum felt that she had not thanked her properly, so she asked Jean for her address so she could send a note of thanks. But Jean had no idea that we had even been in need of food supplies and scolded my mum for not asking for help. She also had no idea who the woman was and neither did anyone else on the street. No one knew of her. I never saw her again.

Was this kind lady an angel? Perhaps! Probably! Possibly! Mum was convinced that she was. All I can remember thinking was, 'Why couldn't Mum have ordered chocolate muffins from the angels?'

Perhaps you are beginning to understand why I believe in angels, but what I witnessed and assimilated in childhood is only half the story. I've also had paranormal experiences of my own as an adult. One of the most dramatic was when the voice of an angel saved my life. I don't want to go over the whole story again if you've already read it in my first angel book, *An Angel Called My Name*, but for those who have not, here is a mini version. I was driving towards a busy junction when I clearly heard the voice of my mother tell me to take a right turning. She had passed several years previously. Unbeknown to me at the time, if I had turned left I would have faced certain death in a back-to-back collision involving two trucks, a stray dog and several vehicles. The accident killed three people – one of whom would have been me if I had turned left as I had fully intended to do before the angel called my name.

After this dramatic celestial rescue my life transformed in many wonderful ways. Previously, although my belief had been strong, I had doubted my own psychic abilities because I'd never actually heard, seen or felt the presence of angels for myself, but after hearing my mother actually communicate to me in spirit, a psychic door opened and I had several other angelic experiences, some of which I shared in my first book and some of which I will share in this book.

Ever since I can remember I've been drawn towards the psychic world and it was a lifetime of dreaming come true when I was eventually given the opportunity to research and write books and encyclopaedias about the paranormal. Then, when several of my books, including *The Element Encyclopedia of 20,000 Dreams*, went on to sell strongly all over the world, my mailbox started to swell with remarkable stories from people worldwide. The great majority of these stories were so positive and uplifting that it became abundantly clear to me that my calling was to gather them together and share them, along with my own experiences, in book form. I could see that I was gently but surely being led on a journey of gathering contemporary accounts of angel experiences from people who wanted to share them.

While writing this book I've been deeply moved by the stories I've read and heard and the generosity of those who have given me permission to share their experiences with you or write their stories up for you. Some of these stories may stretch your belief or even shock you – and in some cases names have been changed to protect identity – but I can assure you that to the best of my knowledge they are all the real deal. In fact, I never fail to be struck by the truth and honesty of the people who send stories in to me.

Having read and heard countless stories from people all over the world, it has become abundantly clear to me that angels are pure beings of goodness and love and you don't need to be an angel expert, clairvoyant, psychic or religious person to see them. The only requirement is an open, trusting heart. It took me until my mid to late thirties to realize that important truth. When I was younger I tried so hard to see angels and to sense the presence of spirits around me, but the harder I tried, the more wretched and abandoned I felt. I didn't realize that all along angels *were* speaking to me but I was too full of fear, self-doubt and guilt to listen.

As you'll see in the thrilling stories that follow, angels speak to us in countless invisible and visible ways: a thought, a feeling, a touch, a smell, a dream, an image or a whisper, book, song, white feather or other astonishing sign. Sometimes they appear in the guise of an animal or a child or in the kindness of strangers. Other times they will manifest through coincidences or through the spirits of loved ones who have passed, and on very rare occasions they also manifest in their familiar form, complete with halo, wings and blinding light.

Today, angels are making their presence known in the world as never before. The internet features hundreds of sites devoted them and thousands of people access those sites every day. There are numerous angel books, newsletters and magazines as well as angel collectibles and memorabilia. In a word, angels are everywhere, but even though they are being taken into people's hearts all over the world it's a sad truth that injustice, poverty, violence and cruelty are still rife. Unfortunately, we live in a world bombarded by images of starving children, terrorists killing innocent people and viruses that can't be cured. The pain and suffering in the world seem to be spiralling out of control. We urgently need to know that there is goodness in and beyond us and that this goodness is more than a match for the pain and hopelessness we see all around us. Therefore there can be no better time for this book to appear to add its voice to the angel movement.

There will always be those who find rational explanations for angelic encounters, but to those who believe, no explanation is necessary. No explanation will ever have the power of the wonderful belief they have. Love is all they need to know, because love is the message that the angels bring.

I truly hope that whether you have had an angel experience or not, reading the amazing stories of ordinary people whose lives have been transformed by angels, as mine was, will be a moving and life-affirming experience. And each time a person is touched or moved by an angel story, the angels fly closer to Earth, spreading more of their pure, unselfish love and goodness in the world.

Above all, I hope that as you read this book you'll be reminded that however tough and complicated life gets, your very own guardian angel is always on your shoulder – a constant, loving presence who wants to assist you. All you need to do is open your mind and your heart to the reality that you are never alone and that both in this life and the next, angels will always be there to lift your heart and give you wings.

But before getting going with these incredible stories, in the first chapter of this book I want to continue a journey I began in my first angel book – the journey of my own psychic adventures. I feel that in order to present, appreciate and interpret the stories of other people not only is it important for me to have had similar experiences myself but also to have understood them. I also feel it is important for my readers to see who I am and where I am coming from.

While it's true that I grew up in a family of psychics and spiritualists and that I've had angelic encounters myself, it's taken a while for me to really believe in the eternal power of goodness and love. I've stumbled a lot on the way, as you'll see in the next chapter, but now I truly believe there is magical potential in everyone and everything, both in this life and the next. I believe there is an angel on my shoulder whenever I work, live and dream, and I'm truly grateful for their loving guidance. Ultimately, I believe in angels not because it is what I was taught to believe or because I have had extraordinary experiences in my life, but because I believe in the power of love. Love is the only language that angels speak and they are all around us – above us, below us, beside us, in front of, behind us and within us. All we need to do is look.

An Angel
on my shoulder

Chapter 1

An Angel on My Shoulder

Angels don't worry about you.
They believe in you.
Author unknown

'If you could just fill out this form,' my health visitor said
with a gentle smile.

'What's it for?' I asked.

'I need to get every new mum to fill one out. It's just
a formality. Just try to answer the questions as truthfully
as you can.'

My tired eyes scanned the form. It was an Edinburgh
post-natal depression survey. I'd filled out one just like
this a year and a half before when my son was born. My
health visitor held out her arms to take my 12-week-old
daughter from me so I could work through the form.
I sat down and glanced quickly through the questions:

Have I been able to laugh or see the funny side of
   things?
Have I blamed myself unnecessarily for things?
Have I felt anxious or worried or scared or panicky for
   no reason?
Have things been getting on top of me?
Have I had difficulty sleeping because of
   unhappiness?
Have I felt sad or miserable?

There were a few others, but they were all pretty similar.
I could clearly see that the questionnaire was trying to
help the health visitor assess the state of my emotional
health.

At first I toyed with the idea of being brutally honest.
Yes, I was feeling tired and unhappy, and I had been
crying myself to sleep at night between feeds, but there
was no way I was going to admit this on a form. Besides,
it was only a phase I was going through and I would
soon shake it off. I'd done my reading and I knew all
about the post-baby blues. I decided it would be far
better to put a positive spin on things – wasn't that what
everyone did? In fact, it felt ridiculous doing the test in
the first place. I wasn't depressed. I wasn't ill or anything.
I wasn't contemplating harming myself or the baby. I was
just feeling a little low. I grabbed a pen and ticked all the
'Hardly ever' options.

As I closed my front door behind the health worker I felt a rush of relief, but that relief was also tinged with disappointment. My mother had always encouraged me to ask for help if I needed it and here I was refusing help when it was offered because I was frightened of being labelled a bad mother. But then I reasoned that I was doing the right thing. What if everything got out of hand and a few tears at bedtime were somehow diagnosed as full-blown post-natal depression? Visions of social workers swooping in and taking my children from me flashed through my mind.

I didn't realize it at the time, but that was the moment when I really started to lose a sense of perspective. My husband was working hard to pay the bills and I was alone with the kids all day and spiralling fast into depression. Neither of us had parents that were alive, and apart from my brother (who was living abroad at the time, so visits were sporadic), we had no close family to give us a break from time to time. Hiring an au pair or nanny was out of the question for me, not just because we were watching the pennies but because I was paranoid about trusting anyone to look after my precious babies. So there I was pretending that life couldn't get any better when in fact I was struggling to keep my head above water.

I Should Have Been Happy

I should have felt on top of the world. OK, we weren't rich in monetary terms, but we were rich in other ways. I had two beautiful children, a 20-month-old son and a newborn baby girl. I had a loving husband and my writing career was coming together. Not only that, but I had been comforted by the presence of my mother in spirit when things hadn't gone to plan during my daughter's birth. The full story is in my first book but, in brief, after years of frustration trying and failing to make contact with the world of spirit, the veil had finally lifted and I'd heard my mother's voice in both my dreams and my waking life. My psychic development had taken a huge leap forward. I really should have been happy. But I wasn't. I felt as if the bottom was about to fall out of my world.

Eight years later I sometimes struggle to understand what happened in those lost dark months following my daughter's birth. Sometimes in the morning when I'm putting on my moisturizer or brushing my teeth I'll still get a flutter of panic. I'll remember how for several long black months I stopped using the cream and brushing my teeth. No point. No time. Then I'll gently put the cream on my cheeks and forehead, feeling comforted by the smooth softness. My tension will ease and any panic will be replaced by a warm glow as I'll remember how at one of the lowest and saddest times of my life my guardian angel walked shoulder to shoulder with me every step of the way.

The first baby I ever held in my arms was my own son. I used to tell people I wasn't very good with babies or 'not that maternal', but the truth was I found the responsibility of babies terrifying. I was scared of doing the wrong thing. I didn't understand what they wanted, I didn't know why they cried, and when I couldn't settle them I would panic and blame myself. I made endless trips to the doctor with my son and each time I was told that he was simply tired, hungry or, in other words, perfectly normal. I read stacks of baby manuals, grateful for any advice I could get from people who seemed to know what to do. I loved and hugged my son, but I also felt sorry for him. I wasn't much of a mother. I'd join play groups and feel that I didn't belong. The other mothers seemed to know everything and do everything right. Nothing I did or said felt right at all.

I just about kept afloat with one child to care for, but when my daughter came along 20 months later I stumbled and slipped. I lived in flip flops, even when it was cold and rainy. There never seemed to be enough time to put proper shoes on, just as there was never time to wear make-up, phone friends or eat properly. I was constantly run down with mouth ulcers, colds and stomach upsets. I felt beaten by the simplest of things. One day my cash card was swallowed up because I'd keyed in my PIN number incorrectly three times. I remember sobbing uncontrollably on the way back home.

I was painfully conscious of my inability to enjoy my children. I'd watch them wriggling their arms and legs and then I'd look at the clock, wondering how long it would be before they napped. And whenever my daughter cried I felt myself spinning out of control. At those moments my anxiety seemed to burst out of my head and force its way into every organ and muscle in my body. Sweat poured off me, my pulse raced, I struggled to get air into my lungs and my stomach filled, as efficiently as a lavatory cistern, with acid.

Not understanding why I couldn't soothe my crying baby or make my toddler son laugh like he did when his dad was around gradually chipped away at my confidence until I had no belief at all in my ability as a mother. I felt a complete failure. This went on for about four months after the birth of my daughter until I experienced perhaps the worst weekend of my life. Then I came crashing down like I'd never known before. I felt weak, I felt like nothing. I wanted to walk away from everything. I was convinced my children would be better off without me. It was the most desperate I had ever felt. I just wanted everything to go away. If I'd seen a truck coming towards me I would have had to fight the impulse to jump in front of it.

After limping through the day I fell into bed that night exhausted but wide awake. As I lay there with tears streaming down my cheeks I realized that for the sake of my children I had to seek help.

I fell into a deep, heavy sleep. I started to dream, but it wasn't like any dream I'd ever had before because I actually knew I was dreaming. It was the weirdest sensation. I couldn't wake up, but I knew I was in control of my dream. I could create anything I wanted. I could be anything I wanted. My first instinct was to fly. I rose in the air without wings. The sense of freedom was intoxicating. I did some cartwheels in the air and laughed at the tiny people below watching me open-mouthed with amazement. My next instinct was to soar. I flew over London. I flew over the ocean. I flew over Disneyland in Florida. I flew into a firework display. I flew to Africa and Egypt and Alaska. Anywhere in the world I wanted to go my dream took me.

I asked my dream to take me to my guardian angel. Curiously, instead of flying up higher to the stars and space, I started to sink down to Earth. It didn't feel as though I was falling, it was as if someone was gently putting me down. I found myself in a field with luscious green grass. There were streams everywhere, bubbling with sparkling water. I heard the sound of a celestial choir and then I saw a figure floating over the grass towards me. Eventually it stopped in front of me, hovering at shoulder height. I think it was female, but I wasn't sure as I couldn't see the face properly because the light was so blinding. I did see golden curls of hair tumbling over shoulders and I also saw wings. They were dazzling blue and when they beat together I felt my whole body shake.

I tried to fly up towards the figure so I could get a better look at the face, but the nearer I tried to fly, the more distant the angel seemed to become. I tried to talk, but no words came out of my mouth. Then I heard a voice speaking. It's hard to describe how it sounded, but the sound of a dozen rushing waterfalls springs to mind. The voice told me that words were not necessary because however far away I seemed my heart's voice could be heard. Then it asked me why I expected motherhood to be easy. There was nothing wrong with things being hard.

Then I felt myself rising higher and higher. I wasn't trying to fly now, I was just floating. I was floating back home, back into my bedroom, back into my sleep, with the words 'perfectly imperfect' echoing through my head.

It must have been about 1 o'clock in the morning when I woke up with a start. I could hear my daughter crying. For a moment I forgot my dream and the weight of sadness still hung heavy on my shoulders, but as I switched my bedside light on with heavy hands and reached for my slippers with aching feet I saw something glistening on the floor beside them. I picked it up. It was a small white feather. Instantly I remembered my dream in vivid, colourful detail. I felt a surge of energy. I went into my daughter's room and picked her up. Her cries turned to sobs. Then I noticed my son sitting up in his bed looking lost and disorientated. I reached out my hand to him and he came running to me.

I tiptoed downstairs with my children. Ignoring all the advice I'd been given, I put my son's favourite Thomas the Tank video on. He squealed with delight. Then I sat down on the sofa and started to feed my daughter. She was ravenous. My son nestled under my arm. As I watched little muscles behind my daughter's ears moving with each swallow and gently stroked my son's dark hair away from his temple I was swept away by a strange disorientating flood of emotion so strong that if I had been standing up I would have collapsed.

'So this is what it feels like to bond with your children,' I thought to myself, amazed. It was as if a flash of insight from my angel dream had opened my eyes. Just because I was struggling to adjust to motherhood didn't mean there was anything wrong with me or that I was an unfit mother. It just meant I was learning, growing up again with my children, as every mother before me had done and every mother after me will do. My angel was right. Becoming a mother, like life itself, wasn't meant to be easy. If everything was easy, how would I ever grow and learn? How would my children ever grow and learn?

About half an hour later my son was asleep and my daughter was babbling quietly to herself. I gently tucked them both back in their beds and went back to mine. As I laid my head down on the pillow, I thanked the angels. For the last few months I'd lost sight of them, but now I could feel them around me again.

Angels. The word lit me up from the inside. It was as though I was hearing it for the first time. There was something tremendous in it, something eternal, something utterly mysterious, yet familiar and important to my life. It was like remembering an incredible secret, one that I had forgotten and shouldn't have. Angels were the key to not just my life, but to everything.

I couldn't sleep. I felt captivated, infatuated and bursting with energy. Out of despair I had prayed for help and out of love my guardian angel had spoken to me and given me hope. I grabbed my laptop and started to surf the internet for angel stories. To my surprise it seemed that the whole world was talking about angels. Although I openly write about the psychic world now, at that time I was still establishing myself as an author and most of my books were in the health, education and popular psychology field. For some reason, I felt I had to be low key about my fascination with the world of spirit. I'm ashamed to admit it, but a part of me was embarrassed about my background and my beliefs.

In the years that followed, whenever I had any spare time I would collect angel stories and interviews and other angel information and put it into a file I called Angel Talk. The file grew so large that I had to create another, and then another. However tired or frazzled I was after a busy day, every time I double clicked on my Angel Talk files I got a tingle of excitement. In my mind's eye I could almost see the stories in book form, but I decided not to approach an editor about a possible book as I would normally have done for the subjects I felt compelled to research in depth. The material was so personal and so astonishing that I knew I had to put my trust in the angels instead and let them decide what should be done with it and when the time was right to present it. In the next few years numerous coincidences and lucid dreams also occurred, as if to remind me of the reality of angels and their very real presence in my life and in the lives of others. So, eight years later, when out of the blue I was asked to write this collection of angel stories by my editor, it felt not only as if the angels were giving me the green light for the project but as if my whole life had been building to this point.

A Loving Presence

I've got a bit ahead of myself, so let's go back to the first year of my daughter's life. In the months after my vivid angel dream there were, of course, times when I felt overwhelmed. What new mother doesn't? But whenever I felt unable to cope or out of my depth all I had to do was remember the feeling of warmth and comfort my guardian angel gave to me that night when I was at such a low ebb. Simply remembering that it was OK to make mistakes and that an angel was walking by my side guiding me through the good times and the bad times was usually enough to give me strength. It wasn't until my daughter's first birthday, however, that the black and heavy fog of depression cleared away completely.

I remember waking up that morning with a violent headache. I'm prone to migraines when I get stressed and that day there was so much to do. Although we had only invited a few friends round and were determined to keep things low key, I still felt apprehensive. This was the first time I had invited a gathering of people to our house since our daughter had been born. A part of me wondered if I was really up to it.

Perhaps I wasn't. For no reason at all, buying the food and drink, wrapping the presents and tidying the house became insurmountable obstacles in my mind. I stood in the shop agonizing over which birthday cake to buy and when I ran out of wrapping paper I cried as if it were a national disaster. On top of all that, the vacuum cleaner wasn't working, so the carpet looked dirty, and the central heating had packed up, so the house felt cold and unwelcoming. But if I'm honest with myself, none of these irritations was the real cause of my distress. The greatest pain for me was that my mother wouldn't be there to celebrate with us. She had always longed for grandchildren but had died before I had got married and had them. She had also died alone.

Regrets

Back in my early twenties I was trying to make my way in the world. I had just landed my first proper job as an editorial assistant for a publisher in London and even though it was a fantastic job, my starting pay was terrible. But as I'd grown up in a low-income household, I was used to making a little go a long way. I rented a tiny box room in an overpriced rundown Hackney bedsit right by a station (so it rattled every few minutes) and made the best of it.

I knew my mum had been ill and constantly fatigued in the last few years, but when she eventually told me she had been diagnosed with bowel cancer, I went into shock and denial. I couldn't cope with it at all. At first I was angry. I thought about it all from my own point of view. Life was hard enough for me starting out on my own in London and I needed my mum's support. I wasn't ready to step into the role of full-time carer yet. I needed the chance to establish my career. And this all felt too grown-up for me.

I went to my doctor for advice. He put me in touch with a hospice. The hospice staff recognized that in a few months my mum would need care 24/7, so offered her a place. This seemed like the best solution, but my mum was having none of it. She point blank refused to leave her home. She wanted to die on her own terms. I understood and respected her wishes, but it left me in a terrible dilemma. I could ask for leave at work, but with doctors estimating that my mum had anywhere between one to five years to live there was no guarantee that my job would be open when I returned. I also wondered what several years caring full time for my mother at home in a tiny Sussex village would do for my employment prospects in the future. There weren't any local jobs in publishing; the place I needed to be was London. This sounds incredibly selfish, but I was young, money was tight and survival mode was kicking in.

I now know that millions of people face the dilemma I faced when loved ones get sick or need round-the-clock care, but back then I felt as if I was the only one. My mum and dad had separated years before and my brother had a new life abroad. I really had no one to turn to. So I decided to compromise and do the best that I could. I would take care of my mum at the weekends but on Monday morning I would make the two-hour journey back to London and organize for a home help to visit and care for her until I returned again on Friday evening. I figured that this arrangement would work in the short term. If my mum's condition deteriorated to the point where she couldn't be left alone I knew I would have to make a drastic lifestyle change, but I didn't really think that would happen. In fact I was convinced she was going to get better. My mum had always been a tower of strength. I had no doubt in my mind she would pull through.

For the next five months I returned home to visit my mum at weekends and every Monday when I left for work I somehow convinced myself that she was making small but steady improvements. I'd tell myself she was keeping down more of her food, staying awake longer and smiling harder. Sometimes she would be incredibly defiant, telling me that she was going to beat this, but other times she would be silent and tearful. Friends and well-wishers offered to help, but my mum refused to see any of them. She didn't want to be a burden to anyone. She even urged me to leave her alone, but I couldn't.

Watching someone you love fade away is an unbearably painful experience. I dealt with it by refusing to accept it was happening. It was impossible for me to admit to myself that she was going to die. But die she did – at 2.11 on a Tuesday afternoon.

She had been weak, jaundiced and fretful on the final Monday morning when I had left at the crack of dawn for work, but I had no reason to suspect that I would never see her again. At her last check-up the doctor had said she was doing as well as could be expected and was not close to the point of death. When the phone call came through to me at work informing me of her death it was like a hammer blow to my heart. It took several weeks for the news to sink in and when the finality of it all hit me, I blamed myself. I was convinced my mum would not have died if I'd been there, and if it really *was* her time to go, at least she would not have died with a home help but with her daughter. How I longed to turn back time and reverse my decision to leave that Monday morning. How I longed to hold my mother's hand and hug her once more.

In the months and years that followed I never stopped berating myself for not being with my mother when she died. I hated myself for putting myself first. Whenever I begged for a sign of forgiveness from her and there was only silence, I was convinced that she was angry with me for deserting her, for not being with her in her hour of need. In my heart of hearts I knew that my mother could never hate me, but I couldn't let my guilt go. The pain came gushing back to me in sporadic waves. Just when I thought I'd come to terms with it, it would come back with such force that it would knock me sideways. And here it was again, years after my mum's death, on my daughter's first birthday. Once again it was blunting my joy and chipping away at my confidence.

With about an hour to go before the guests arrived, I stared at my daughter's birthday cake and thought about my mother's final lonely moments. I kept my hands busy by tidying the house, but this didn't keep my mind busy and I remembered my mother crying the last few times I'd left her. Why hadn't I stayed with her? I tried to pull myself together, but my mother's tearful and disappointed face overwhelmed me. My grief and hurt became so intense that I found it hard to breathe. I walked outside, hoping that a gust of fresh air would help release the tension inside.

It was a cold but beautiful afternoon with the promise of a warmer evening ahead. The sun was shining brightly in the sky and as I looked up I closed my tearful eyes for a moment to escape the glare. When I opened them, the sight that met my gaze was breathtaking. There, in the centre of the sky, was a cloud in the shape of an angel. It was perfect in every detail, especially the wings, which seemed to spread right from the top of the head to the bottom of the billowing gown. The hands were folded as if in prayer. What made the whole thing even more remarkable was this particular cloud was stationary and clear white, whereas the clouds around it were moving. It was also the only definite cloud shape I could see in the sky.

I'd often read about angels appearing in the guise of clouds, but this was the first time I'd seen one for myself. I knew then that my mum had forgiven me. I also knew that she had never been angry with me in the first place. A deep sensation of peace filled me and the burden of guilt that had weighed heavily on my heart all those years lifted. Here at last was the sign of forgiveness I had been looking for.

The cloud remained so clear for such a long time that it will be forever etched in my memory. When it eventually dissolved I walked into my house with a spring in my step and there, right in the centre of the kitchen table, was a mug with 'World's Greatest Mum' written on it. I had no memory of placing it there and to this day don't know how it got there, as there was no one in the house at the time. I'd been given it about a year or so before by my husband, but had never used it. I had felt unworthy of the accolade and had packed it away in a dark corner of one of my kitchen cupboards. But here it was, ready to use, without a speck of dust on it.

I put the kettle on to make a cup of tea and as I sat down to enjoy it with a couple of digestive biscuits I started to giggle. In my mind I could hear my mum saying with a hint of laughter in her voice that the mug was for her, not me! I knew that she was going to be present in spirit at my daughter's first birthday party.

The years have flown by since I saw my perfect cloud angel and met my guardian angel in my dreams. My children are ten and eight now, but every moment with them is a precious gift – even those 'not so perfect' moments when tempers fly and doors are slammed. Everything my guardian angel told me in my dream is true. As long as we grow emotionally and spiritually, it's OK to have weaknesses, to make mistakes and to do all the other things that make us human. I'll never be the perfect mother, or the perfect human being, but I understand what my angel was telling me – that human perfection is about being imperfect. My children don't want or need the perfect mother; they need a mother who loves them and who isn't afraid to learn from her mistakes, and grow up again with them.

A Door Opens

Discovering that I was capable of experiencing such overwhelming feelings of peace triggered other amazing psychic experiences. My dreams became even more vivid and colourful, to the point where I was able not only to lucid dream at will – that is, to know I was dreaming – but also to travel out of body. (There's more about my night-time adventures – and in case you're wondering I mean this in a spiritual not a physical sense – in Chapter Five, Night Visions.) But it wasn't just in my dreams that I saw angels – I felt their presence in my waking life too.

One occasion stands out in particular. My children were two and four and I was waiting with them at a bus stop when a couple of drunken men started to harass us. I was backed into a corner and with a double stroller it was hard for me to move away from them quickly. As their language became more menacing and threatening I glanced at the cars flashing past in the street and prayed for someone to notice what was going on.

Moments later, a blue limo pulled up on the opposite side of the road. I remember thinking that I hadn't seen a blue limo before. The door opened and a blonde fair-skinned woman in a dark blue suit leaned out and said quietly, 'Leave her alone.' The drunken men turned away from me and started to walk towards the car, at which point the woman closed her door and drove off. The drunks kept stumbling along behind her as if they were in a trance. I watched them walk off into the distance. I kept hoping the woman would come back and offer us a lift, because it took another 20 minutes before the bus arrived, but she never did. Whether she was an angel or a human guided by an angel I'm not sure, but I have never forgotten her, or her shiny blue limo.

The Flashing Cursor

I also believe that angels look over my shoulder as I work. I love what I do, but when I first decided to take the plunge and put my steady teaching and journalistic work aside and go freelance as an author, many of my colleagues and friends told me it was unwise as I'd never be able to earn a living. They were right. A book contract back then was like gold dust. I was strongly advised to get an agent, but I never needed one. After countless rejections I got my first contract for a book about health and that book led to another and another. And over the past eight years I've never been out of work.

It wasn't until a few years ago, however, that I was finally given the chance to write about what I am truly passionate about – the paranormal. It wasn't too much of a leap from health and popular psychology, because in my mind the only way for a person to feel truly happy and fulfilled is to be healthy in body, mind and spirit. I have to admit, though, that although I was thrilled to be asked I was also rather apprehensive. I knew that some people would think I was crazy, especially my old student friends and tutors from Cambridge, who had made it clear to me during my student days that they were highly sceptical of my belief in life after death. I knew I was putting my credibility as a non-fiction author on the line. But as my first paranormal book assignment was an encyclopaedia about the psychic world and my task was to present an objective voice, I didn't think my decision would be too heavily criticized. Fortunately, that encyclopaedia went on to become a success, as did subsequent ones, and that success gave me the opportunity to write this book. When my editor called to ask me if I had any angel stories to tell, without hesitation I told her that I had enough to fill a library.

With the contract signed, I sat down in front of my PC to begin my first angel book. I opened up a blank document and stared at the cursor flashing on the screen. Though I felt tremendous happiness to be doing this work, I also had butterflies in my stomach. I had never written about my personal experiences of the paranormal before. I'd also never been entrusted with writing up the intimate personal stories of other people, so this was my greatest challenge to date as an author. I wondered if I was up to the task; self-doubt began to creep in. I needed to know if I could do this. I decided to ask my guardian angel for a sign.

I focused deep inside myself and asked my guardian angel to give me an answer. I concentrated long and hard. I poured my heart out with all the honesty, courage and conviction I could find. Then I waited for an answer. There was nothing. I waited again. Still there was nothing. I looked again at the cursor flashing on the screen. It was flashing impatiently and angrily at me. The angels clearly weren't going to reassure me. Did they simply want me to get on with it?

I started to tentatively write down some thoughts. They were disjointed and confused at first, but at least they were a start. Then I dug out my Angel Talk files and mailbox and started to transfer stories. I was starting to create a book. I read through a few paragraphs and enjoyed what I was reading. Encouraged, I kept on writing. The words flowed.

After a few hours I glanced at my watch and realized I'd been working for three hours without a break. Time had flown by. I went into the kitchen to make a cup of tea, but the kettle wasn't working. I tried the lights and it was the same. We'd had a power cut. I went back to my office. My computer had powered down and there was no power to switch it on. It was then that I panicked. I'd never had a power cut before, so hadn't got into the habit of saving my work every few pages. Worse still, I didn't think I'd even saved it at all. My entire morning had been wasted. Were the angels sending me the message that the book wasn't a good idea?

Half an hour later the power came back on. Fearing the worst, I switched on my PC and to my delight all my angel files were there just as I had left them. I resumed my work on the book with a new peace of mind.

The most remarkable thing about this experience, though, is that later I found out that my house had lost power not at 1 p.m. when I went into my kitchen to make a cuppa, but at 10.30 a.m. Somehow, when all the other electrical appliances in my house had lost power, my computer had kept on running, allowing me to work uninterrupted. Sure, it's possible that it had gone into battery mode, but for me there was no mistaking that the angels were sending me a message loud and clear. Once again they had shown me that when you start to acknowledge their presence in your life, you start to notice them everywhere, in everything – even a flashing cursor.

Chapter 2

In the Arms of an Angel

See, I am sending an angel ahead of you
to guard you along the way.

Exodus 23:20

I can imagine what angels might look like from my dreams and from images I've seen in clouds or in paintings and from the hundreds of accounts of people who have seen them. But in my waking life I have never actually had a traditional angel encounter complete with blinding light, wings and halo or felt the brush of angel wings on my skin. Still I know, without a doubt, that angels exist and are here to help us.

When I was growing up in a household of psychics and spiritualists I often felt frustrated and inadequate because I didn't seem to have inherited the 'gift'. I attended many psychic development classes and workshops where fellow students would see visions of inspiration and brilliance. I, however, would sit in darkness, feeling peaceful but hearing and seeing nothing. It wasn't until my thirties that these channels started to gradually open for me and even now I can't predict when they will do so because on every occasion when I have had an angelic encounter it has been spontaneous. I still can't summon, see, hear or feel angels and spirits like a seasoned psychic or medium can, but this has not in any way dampened my belief in angels and their guidance. This is because over the years I have learned that, like everyone else, I see, hear and experience angels in my own unique way. Looking back, I can see that angels were helping me throughout my life. I just wasn't aware of it at the time.

In this chapter I've gathered together a collection of stories which show just some of the many mysterious and dramatic ways in which angels can intervene in our lives, and what's interesting is that not one of the people who contributed these stories believes themselves to be psychic or clairvoyant. They are simply ordinary people whose lives have been transformed by something extraordinary. Let's begin with Sandra's dramatic and moving story:

Vanilla Ice Cream

I hardly know where or how to begin this story. It's been such a long road with so many twists and turns.

For many years I had a charmed life. I was born into a loving family. We weren't millionaires, but we had plenty of money. I was popular at school and head girl in my last year. I got into the college of my choice and it wasn't much of a struggle getting a job I loved or finding and falling in love with the right man. I was also fit and healthy and apart from the odd bout of 'flu had never been really ill. Like most people, I never thought about my mortality seriously. I felt invincible. By the time I was 34 years old, my job was great and my husband supportive and loving and I was the mother of a beautiful healthy three-year-old boy called Riley. Little did I know that my reality was about to change as abruptly as if I had crashed into a brick wall while travelling at 90 miles an hour.

When Riley was born I had had a minor scare when some of my breast milk ducts had blocked, but an inspection had given me the all-clear. I remember my doctor telling me to continue to inspect my breasts regularly and I said I would but I didn't. I didn't think that 30 year olds could get breast cancer and besides there wasn't a history of it in my family. But then few years later I noticed a soreness and lumpiness on the underside of my left breast. After reluctantly agreeing to a mammogram, I was diagnosed with breast cancer.

When I left my doctor's office after the diagnosis my legs felt weak. My husband was holding my hand, but

I had never felt so alone or so abandoned. I was convinced that I was going to die. We drove home in silence, punctuated only by the sounds of our sobs. When I arrived home, Riley greeted me with his usual enthusiasm. I picked him up and crushed him to me with tears streaming down my face. He struggled to free his hands and then started to wipe the tears from my face. 'Don't worry, Mama,' he said, 'the vanilla ice-cream lady says you'll be fine. You're ill, but you've got to fight.'

I hugged my son again and put him down, flashing an angry look at my au pair, as I had expressly asked her not to tell Riley that I was going to the doctor or to give him ice cream. She shook her head and shrugged her shoulders and silently mouthed, 'I haven't said anything,' to me. But Riley was still chuckling and talking about the vanilla ice-cream lady. Even though my heart was crying, I found myself smiling at his babbling and asked who the vanilla-cone lady was. My son laughed and pointed behind me and told me she was there right behind me. I looked behind me and there was no one there. My son was obviously going through an imaginary friend stage. I hugged him tightly, but he kept on pointing behind me and saying the vanilla-cone lady was watching and she wanted me to fight. I thought he was talking nonsense, but as I hugged him I felt lighter. My son had told me to fight and that word echoed around my head. I felt a bolt of energy, like electricity, surge through me. Other people had beaten cancer – why couldn't I? I had a family to care for, a child to raise and a life to live. From that moment on I began an all-out war which would last nearly three years and include a modified radical mastectomy, chemotherapy and even a bone-marrow transplant.

Through all this, friends and family flocked to our side. It's amazing how people respond when others are in need and I learned much about the innate goodness of people and how essential sharing love is to the human experience. Slowly I began to feel hope, and this hope gave me strength. The possibility of miracles and the wonder of life became everyday ideas to me. I began to question my thought patterns more. I pondered why I thought it was more realistic to expect a negative outcome than a positive one. I made the decision to opt for the positive and this was one of the most important factors in my well-being.

I was weak from chemotherapy the night an angel lifted me in its arms. At that time not only did I require a wheelchair to go from place to place, but the rest of the time I was confined to bed. I had spent seven weeks in isolation in hospital while doctors tried to figure out how to treat my blood counts, which had dropped dangerously low and seemed insistent upon remaining there. One night – it must have been about 11 p.m. as the nurse had done her final rounds for the night – I lay there feeling weak, sick and tired. I tried to grasp onto some hope, but it slipped through my fingers. I felt as though I had reached the end of the road. A part of me hoped that when I went to sleep I wouldn't wake up. Yes, I was a fighter, but every good fighter knows when they are beaten. I closed my eyes and tried to swallow, but there wasn't even enough saliva in my throat to let me do that.

I closed my eyes harder and saw Riley's smiling face. The pain of not being able to see him grow up was so intense I could feel vomit burning in my throat. And then, with the image of my son still in my mind, the scent of vanilla ice cream filled the air. I suddenly felt warmth and the pain that wracked my body disappeared. Then I felt a pair of arms lift me gently and suddenly I was floating a few inches from my bed. I saw many bright colours, a white star and an exquisite white light. I also saw an intensely beautiful violet light – a violet I had never seen before. I felt invisible hands stroking my forehead. I didn't see or hear anything, but I sensed the presence of love and joy. It felt as though there was a party going on all around me. I wanted to get up and join in the fun. My heart opened wide with an intense surge of hope. It was an enchantingly beautiful experience. The only other time in my life that I can remember feeling a little like this was immediately after I had given birth to my son.

All too soon I heard the voice of an angel – it sounded like a woman's but it could have been a man's – saying, 'You're done.' I felt myself being gently lowered back to the bed and then the lights and the sensation were gone. I looked around and pinched myself. This had not been a dream.

In the weeks that followed, angels visited me several times. I would know when they were about to arrive because the most heavenly scent of vanilla ice cream would fill the air. Even though I often felt weak and drained when they came to me, each time I felt again the energy of my life. It was like the buzz or hum of my being.

When I finally left hospital to go home the doctors were amazed at the speed of my recovery. Sadly, the angels didn't visit me while I recovered at home, but nevertheless after another six months I was finally given the all-clear. In my heart I knew the angels leaving was their way of telling me that I was ready to fully recover on my own, that I was ready to care for myself and my family the way I always had.

Within a year I was once again the busy, energetic, healthy person I had been before the cancer, but even though I may have looked the same I didn't feel the same. My life had a depth and a richness I had never known before.

I didn't tell anyone, not even my husband, about my angelic experiences, but I did ask Riley about the vanilla-cone lady. He told me that she didn't visit him anymore. I told him not to be sad because even though he couldn't see her I was sure she was still watching over us.

I am now 47 years old. As I said, it's been a long journey. My cancer was a terrifying experience, but I will always cherish the lessons I learned about myself – and life – as a result of it. And it will always be my privilege to feel both happy and sad whenever I smell vanilla ice cream – happy in that I know my guardian angel is watching over me and sad in that it took a life-threatening illness for me to recognize her loving presence.

Sandra truly believes that her guardian angel helped her overcome a devastating illness but, as David's story shows, it isn't just physical illness that can be healed by an angelic encounter. Angels are master healers of the heart.

'Open your Eyes'

Ever since I can remember I wanted to be a doctor. I remember how I buzzed with excitement and adrenalin the first day I spent on the wards. But after my wife died – she was a doctor too – a part of me died. I turned up for work every morning, but it was as if I was going through the motions. I realized that although I loved my job, I loved my wife more.

We had met in the hospital canteen four years before. I had been so tired after a night shift that my breakfast tray had slipped out of my hands. Food had gone everywhere. What a mess. It was embarrassing, too, but Sarah – that was her name – just giggled. It really broke the tension. She helped me clean up and we got on instantly. After that I started to look out for her in the mornings and we'd have a quick chat and a giggle. I realized I was falling in love with her when she didn't show up one morning and I felt out of sorts all day. The next time I saw her I asked her out and we were married 18 months later.

We'd only been married a year when she died. She was fine in the morning, but in the afternoon she kept complaining of headaches. I didn't think much of it because when you're a doctor headaches – along with bags under the eyes – are part of the job. She went to work as usual and then I got a phone call telling me she had died of a cerebral haemorrhage.

As a doctor I'd given people news like this on many occasions, but it's a whole different ball game when it happens to you. For the next few days I was literally numb. I couldn't cry. I couldn't think. I just busied myself with the funeral arrangements. I was told to take time off work, but that was the last thing I wanted. I needed to be distracted. So two weeks after the death of my wife I was back at work.

I guess it was about four months after Sarah died that denial was replaced by grief. I can't say what the trigger was, because there wasn't one. I was doing my rounds one morning and then it hit me like a bullet. My legs felt weak and I nearly passed out. Colleagues ushered me away to an office as I sobbed uncontrollably. My wife had been everything to me. I didn't think I could live without her. I must have sobbed for hours that afternoon. I can't remember much about it, but I was told that I was found curled up in a corner of the office singing to myself. I simply can't remember it.

What I do remember is that the next two months of my life were harrowing ones. I was given a month's leave and I spent almost all of it locked up in my flat. I don't think I ate, but I drank far too much. Physically there was nothing wrong with me, but my heart was smashed to pieces.

Three years later I was still getting severe episodes of grief that came over me without warning but they weren't as frequent as they had been at the beginning of my mourning. I learned to cope with them by shutting myself away and spending the rest of my life on automatic. I wouldn't let anyone get close to me. I was rude and bitter to friends and family. I didn't want to know. Eventually they gave up and stopped calling. The only thing that got me up in the morning was my job. To numb the pain I worked harder than ever.

One morning I was driving home after a 20-hour shift listening to the car radio when I felt my eyelids grow heavy. I was so familiar with the feeling of barely being able to keep my eyes open that it didn't bother me. Besides, I had driven to and from work so often it was if

I could do that journey on automatic. Then, as I turned a corner, I heard a clatter. It sounded like a tray clattering to the floor and I was instantly reminded of the time I met my wife. I'd been exhausted then too. Tears stung my eyes and I put my foot down on the accelerator to distract myself by driving faster. I looked in the mirror to see if there was any traffic behind me and there in the passenger seat I saw my wife as plain as day. She smiled and blinked several times and then said in the voice I knew and loved, 'Open your eyes.' Then she giggled and looked back at the road. I screwed up my eyes in disbelief and when I opened them up again she had gone.

Wide awake now, I put my foot on the brake to slow down, and as I did so, oncoming traffic rushed by. I realized that without Sarah's warning I would most likely have run off the road or straight into the oncoming traffic. She had woken me up while I was asleep at the wheel and saved my life.

I've never told a soul about what happened to me that night on the motorway but it was a lifesaver in so many ways. I still miss Sarah terribly, but there is no doubt in my mind that she is watching over and guiding me and on that morning she saved my life. Clearly she wants me to live my life to the full. This Christmas I'll be spending it with my brother and his family. I'm not ready for anything more yet, but one day I'm sure my heart will be ready to share again. In the meantime I feel that my experience has enriched me both as a person and as a doctor. For one thing, telling partners and relatives about the death of a loved one isn't as painful an experience as it used to be because I know that death is not the end and that if we remember them with our hearts, the people we love never die.

Like David, Marcia, who tells us her story below, suffered deeply with grief, confusion and a sense of emptiness when she lost her only son, Jack, in an accident. And, again like David, a visit from the afterlife gave her not just strength and comfort but a new lease of life. Here's her incredible story:

Für Elise

No mother expects to bury her son. Jack was my only son and my hope for the future. I was a single parent and it was just the two of us as he was growing up. I spoiled him rotten, but I couldn't help it. He was adorable. I never got much love and care when I was a child. My mother gave me up for adoption at the age of two – she was a drug addict apparently – and I grew up in care. So when Jack came along I was determined to give him everything I never had. I worked long and hard to send him to private school and when he showed a talent for music I paid for piano lessons. He was really gifted. I remember when he was only eight he played *Für Elise* with such wonderful touch and depth that he won first prize in a local music competition. There were over 30 competitors and he was the youngest entrant.

When Jack left school along with a string of 'A' grades at A-level he applied to a prestigious music academy. I felt as if my heart would burst with pride when I heard the news that he'd been accepted. He never made it to college, though. He died three days before he was due to start his course. He'd begged me for a motorbike but I'd thought it was too dangerous, so eventually we'd agreed on buying him a second-hand car. He'd only just passed his test when he was involved in a fatal collision on a roundabout. Apparently he swerved to avoid hitting a car full on, but in the process his car jammed right into the railings. He died instantly. I can't help wondering if I'd allowed him to have a motorbike he'd still be alive today.

I could hardly take in the news when the policemen came knocking at my door to tell me. It was impossible for me to think of my Jack, my talented, fun-loving Jack, the centre of my world, as dead. I don't know how I made it through the first few weeks. It was like a nightmare. It felt unreal and I longed to wake up and find that everything was back to normal. The hardest part was not having the opportunity to say goodbye. There were days when I was quite literally numb with grief. Friends tried to comfort me by telling me Jack was at peace in the afterlife but I'd always believed that death was the end and when some-one died that was it. So I knew Jack was gone, but every day – sometimes several times a day – I'd wander over to the cemetery. I just had this overwhelming need to be with him. Even though I didn't believe in an afterlife I couldn't accept that he was dead. I'd spend hours chatting away to him by his grave.

On one particularly dark evening I decided to go to bed early. Sleeping was hard and I took a few pills to help me. I heard the phone ringing but decided to ignore it. I didn't have much interest in anyone or anything. I tried to sleep, but much to my frustration the pills didn't seem to be working. I was still wide awake when I heard the phone ringing again. It was more persistent this time and I counted up to 30 rings. Nevertheless there was no way I was going to answer it. If someone wanted to speak to me they could speak in the morning. About half an hour later, when I heard it ringing again, I put my head under the pillow to blank out the noise. As I did so I heard the faint tinkling of piano music. It was *Für Elise*. I sat bolt upright. The piano playing was even louder and it sounded as if the music was coming from downstairs.

I clutched onto the banisters as I went downstairs. Yes, there was no doubt about it – the music was coming from Jack's piano in the front room. I opened the door, half-expecting to see him sitting there. He wasn't there and the notes on the piano were not moving, but still I could hear the music. I walked towards the piano and suddenly the music stopped ringing in my ears. In its place I heard the telephone ringing again. I was standing right by it. Hardly knowing what I was doing I was in such a daze, I picked it up.

'Hello,' said a male voice on the other end of the phone.

I didn't reply. I was still in shock about the piano music.

'This is hard for me and I know it will be hard for you but I've been trying to get in touch with you for days now,' said the gentle but strong voice. 'Please don't be shocked or frightened, as I promise not to disturb you if this isn't what you want, but I'd really like to meet you. You see, I'm your twin brother, Jack.'

'Brother,' I mumbled. 'I have a brother? My son was called Jack.'

'Yes, I only heard a few weeks ago about your terrible loss. I don't want to intrude, as this is a vulnerable time for you, but I'd like to be there for you or help if I can.'

The following week I did meet up with my brother Jack. It was an emotional reunion for us both. I'd had no idea I had any siblings, let alone that I was a twin. I also found out that my brother had two children of his own. I'm an auntie. Nothing will ever replace my Jack, but I have a family again.

Apart from the amazing coincidence that both my son and my brother were called Jack, I am convinced that

I was guided to the phone that night by Jack's spirit. He clearly wanted me to pick up the phone and speak to my brother. And although there were no bright lights and no spirit to be seen, hearing Jack play the piano again filled my heart with unimaginable joy because I knew that my amazing son had not gone far away at all.

Denial and depression are perfectly natural defence mechanisms following the death of a loved one. Everyone works through the stages of grief in their own special way, but in most cases denial is replaced by anger, followed by despair and then eventually acceptance. In Lisa's case, however, the experience of grief and loss led her on a dangerously self-destructive path.

'How Will I Ever Cope?'

My mother and I were wonderfully close. I could talk to her about anything. She was my rock. When she died suddenly of a heart attack I felt like a ship without an anchor. I was 30 at the time, but emotionally I was about 15. As I watched her coffin being lowered into the ground at her funeral all I could think was, 'How will I ever cope without you?'

Not knowing where to turn for support, I drowned my grief by investing all my energy and need for comfort and love into men. I had a series of boyfriends, each more useless than the last, but however badly they treated me I kept running back for more. I was terrified of being alone. It was too painful without being able to call Mum.

When I first met Dan he was charming. I thought I loved him and I devoted myself to him. But after a few weeks he stopped being charming and started being violent. If I'd had enough self-esteem I would have left instantly, but I didn't. The odd slap and shove soon turned to the odd kick and thump and then one night he got really savage. I don't remember much after that but when I woke up I was lying on the kitchen floor and I couldn't see anything because blood was covering my eyes. Every part of my body ached, but the place I hurt the most was in my heart. I started to cry and the tears cleared my vision. I put my thumb in my mouth and began to gently rock myself.

At that instant the atmosphere in my kitchen seemed to change and I felt my mum's presence. I didn't see her or hear her, but I knew she was beside me. I was filled with a sensation of love. I felt strong arms gently encircling me and holding me tight. There was no one in the room with me at the time and in my mind I know it was my mum. She was telling me that I was not and never would be alone.

All this happened five years ago, but I can still close my eyes and remember the feeling of being held gently in my mum's arms. Her love that day gave me the incentive I needed to leave Dan and report him to the police. Her love gave me the courage I needed to stay away from destructive relationships. Today my life is full, even though I am not in a relationship. I feel strong and optimistic. I'm not afraid of being by myself anymore because I'm confident in the knowledge that my mum is always with me and I'm never alone.

Lisa's story is similar to many others I have collected over the years in which the spirit of a lost loved one returns briefly to offer strength in times of crisis. The return typically only lasts a split-second, but it is long enough to bring comfort and hope for the future. These stories are a source of great comfort because they show that even though we may not always see them, angels are with us during times of need.

After being told that her five-year-old son, Thomas, had slipped into a coma, Sheila felt a magical, loving presence which gave her the courage and the strength she had previously lacked.

Quietly Slipping Away

I was inconsolable when my five-year-old son Thomas went into a coma. The doctors told me the meningitis had taken a firm hold. His chances of survival depended on how strong his little body's immune system was, but the prognosis was not good. There was little chance of him ever waking up again and I was told that he was quietly slipping away.

How could I ever get past this and go on? I didn't know if I had the strength. I sat by my son's bed. It was getting dark outside and inside. I felt numb. I sat there and waited.

At around 9 p.m. Thomas started to twitch. Then he opened his eyes and started to say in a weak voice, 'Mummy, I want to stay with you. I'm frightened. The angels want me to come with them.'

I lay down beside Thomas in his bed and held and kissed him. I'm not religious, but I begged the angels to let me keep my son. I pleaded and I sobbed, but deep down I knew that this was a battle I didn't have any say in.

I looked at Thomas again. His eyes were closed again but he was smiling. I knew this was it and I couldn't accept it. I picked Thomas up and held him to me, ignoring all the tubes and equipment. As I held him, his little life flashed through my head in pictures. I saw him kicking his first football, stamping his foot when I wouldn't give him seconds, laughing when I blew on his stomach. Then I saw in my head all the things I wanted to see him doing when he got older. I saw him riding a bike, playing in the school football team, running with a kite. I longed with all my heart to see him grow up, but there was nothing I could do. I was helpless. So I did the only thing I could – I held him tight.

After several minutes holding my son's limp body in my hands I felt as if someone was standing right behind me. I felt a wonderful sense of peace and strength and I knew in that instant that I would have the strength to cope. A sense of calm came over me. I immediately stopped crying and I pictured my son happy and healthy again with the angels in heaven.

I turned around, expecting to see my mum or a doctor there trying to console me, but there was no one there. I believe that it was my guardian angel standing behind me giving me a wonderful sense of peace and hope.

Thomas remained unconscious for the rest of the night but the following morning he shocked everyone, especially me, as I was convinced he had quietly slipped away in the night, when he opened his eyes. The infection that had raged through his body was gone. He looked into my eyes and said, 'I love you, Mummy,' and then he looked up at the ceiling and said, 'I love you too, angel.'

I stroked my son's hands and face. The happiness and gratitude in my heart felt too much to bear. The angels had listened to the heartfelt longings of an ordinary boy and his mother.

Yes, I believe in angels, but not because of the miracle of my son's life. After I felt the loving, magical touch of an angel standing behind me I would have believed in angels whatever the outcome.

If we just open our hearts and our minds, angels can bring comfort, peace and healing at the best and worst of times. Here's Grace's story:

'Remember?'

'Where are my spectacles?' my dad said, looking confused.

'They're on the top of your head,' I replied. 'You just pushed them there a moment ago, remember?'

Dad shrugged his shoulders, slipped his spectacles onto his nose and buried his head again in the paper. I bought him a cup of tea and he pushed his spectacles on his head to drink it. I went back into the kitchen but turned back again as he was shouting for me.

'Grace! Grace! Have you seen my spectacles?'

'Dad!' I replied. 'You just asked me that. They're on the top of your head, just as they were a moment ago.'

Dad nodded, but he still looked puzzled, and this worried me. Although he was only in his early sixties ever since he had retired he had started to forget things. I'd read about memory loss with age so I decided to encourage him to do some crosswords every day. I also thought about buying him a Nintendo for Christmas so he could do some brain-training exercises.

Then a few weeks later I asked him to pick up my sons, Tom, eleven, and Jack, six, from school. I phoned him in the morning to remind him and he promised he'd be there, but at 4 p.m. I got a phone call from Tom's form teacher asking when Tom and Jack were going to be picked up. I phoned Dad and he was at home listening to the radio. He couldn't remember speaking to me in the morning.

A month or so later I got a phone call at work from my next-door neighbours. They had spotted my dad sitting on the floor in our local shopping centre. When they had gone up to him to ask if he was OK he'd had no idea who they were and had started to shout abuse at them. It was terrible seeing my dad deteriorate like this.

It wasn't long before Dad was diagnosed with the early stages of Alzheimer's. There were days when he was completely normal but there were also days when he would leave his house and just wander for miles with no idea where he was going. I was concerned for his safety and so he moved in with me and my husband Ben. This arrangement just about worked for 18 months but then Dad started to behave really erratically. Night times were the worst. He would drift around the house rearranging the furniture. He also became incontinent and started to shout at the children and call them names.

I staggered on for the next two years as best I could, but by the time my dad was 65 I was getting desperate. My biggest concern was for the safety of my children, especially now that Dad was lighting matches for no reason. I asked for help from my doctor, but the more

I asked, the more tests my dad was sent for and the more forms I had to fill in. I felt trapped.

By this time my dad found it hard to even remember my name. He'd look at me as if I were a stranger, or an enemy. One night when I was trying to get him to rest he started shouting and accusing me of kidnapping him. It took four hours to settle him and I fell into bed in the small hours of the morning, totally burned out. I was so tired that I couldn't sleep and I just lay there crying. Ever since I'd left school I'd been busy working and earning money and raising a family. I'd stopped thinking about or believing in any higher power, but that night I begged for someone to help me and to help my dad.

All of a sudden I saw a light ball flicker beside my bed. I rubbed my eyes to make sure I wasn't seeing things and crawled to the bottom of my bed to take a closer look. Then I saw an angel. It was fairly small, about the size of a football, and it was just floating at the bottom of the bed. It had bright golden wings and a long gown that sparkled with light. It was the most beautiful thing I have ever seen and as I gazed at it in wonder the most amazing feeling of peace came over me.

The angel floated towards me and I felt all the tension leave my body and warmth come over me. The angel hovered in front of me for a few minutes and then it vanished. I knew then that everything was going to work out fine.

My husband was asleep the whole time. I know it wasn't a hallucination because from that night onwards it felt as if a weight had lifted off my shoulders. The next morning social services called and I was told that a home help would be visiting for a couple of hours every day to give me a break. It meant I could start to get my life back together again.

For the next three years Dad's condition got steadily worse and in the last six months of his life he didn't recognize me at all. Despite this I still felt that there was a strong connection between us and sometimes he would look at me as if he knew what I was thinking. I also felt his love for me. The day before he died he woke up and raised his arms towards me. When I came over he looked at me and said my name. I longed for him to say more, but really my name was enough. My dad had remembered me at last. The next day he slipped into unconsciousness and passed away gently in his sleep.

Although my dad's illness weighed heavily on his family, my guardian angel gave me the strength I needed to cope when I was at my lowest. She opened my eyes to the world of spirit and this made losing Dad so much easier to bear.

Life can certainly bring us many challenges, and at times these challenges can seem impossible to bear, but it isn't just during times of danger or extreme crisis that angels can make their watchful presence felt. In the remarkable stories that follow angels appeared spontaneously in the most ordinary but unusual ways. Let's begin with Martin's experience.

For Sale

In the late 1980s my wife and I were trying to get our feet on the property ladder. She was a midwife and I was a fireman and we both worked long hours with little financial reward. We were sort of coping with the bills until my wife got pregnant with twins. It was the most amazing news but I had no idea how we could manage on our pay packets. At the time we were renting a tiny flat and as the months ticked away slowly the pressure to move out and find a proper home to start a family in was intense.

Every weekend we'd look around house after house, but each time they were either too expensive or too far away from our work. With just two months to go before I became a dad I started to get really worried. I scanned the newspapers and signed up for agencies, but there was nothing suitable. We came close to finding somewhere on one occasion but eventually lost out because I couldn't get the deposit together in time.

One Saturday afternoon I got a phone call from a mate at work saying there was a house for sale a couple of streets away from him that might be worth checking out.

On the off-chance that someone might be in to let us view it, I raced round immediately. It was a lovely little detached house in a quiet cul de sac with a park a few blocks away. As I walked up the drive I imagined myself mowing the lawn while my wife smiled at me from the kitchen.

I rang the doorbell and a man answered. He must have been in his sixties or early seventies and he introduced himself as Doug. He was more than willing to show us around. There were three spacious bedrooms and a bathroom upstairs and a roomy kitchen, study and living room downstairs. The back garden was delightful and I complimented Doug on his flowerbeds. He chuckled and told me that he'd spent years getting the garden the way he wanted it. He said it had been a wilderness when he'd arrived and asked me to make sure that I took care of it in the same way when I lived there. I was surprised that he assumed I would be living here and asked him if other people had viewed the property. He said there had been four or five others but he wanted me to have the house. He told me to come round the following morning to meet his daughter and start the legal process. I asked him about a deposit and he said I wasn't to worry. We'd sort something out in the morning. The house was ours.

Doug showed me to the door and as we said goodbye he took a pen out of his pocket. He asked me to give it back to his daughter the next day because he had borrowed it from her and had not given it back. I took the pen, which had the name 'Alice' engraved on it, and shook his hand firmly, promising him that I'd take care of his house. I was so excited that the oddness of it all didn't really strike me until I was walking home. He'd said he wouldn't be able to see us the next morning, but in that case why didn't he just leave the pen for his daughter in her house?

When I went home that night I told my wife about what had happened. We didn't allow ourselves to get our hopes up, though, as we had had them dashed so many times before and without anything written in stone we knew that Doug's promise to us might not hold up. All the same, the next morning we went to meet Doug's daughter with high hopes. I was due to start my shift later that day, so I had my uniform on.

A woman in her thirties opened the door and we introduced ourselves. I asked her if her name was Alice and she nodded. I told her that her father had shown us around the house yesterday and agreed to let us buy it. I told her that he had been very particular about the garden. I also handed her the pen he had asked me to give her. She didn't say a word the whole time and I apologized for not giving her a moment to speak, but told her it was because we were so thrilled. Then I paused and waited for her to respond, but she just stood there staring at us. I asked her if she was OK and she nodded and gestured for us to step inside.

When we went inside I got a sinking feeling and started to think that perhaps Doug was suffering from dementia and this was all a terrible misunderstanding. I was just about to make my apologies when Alice asked us if we wanted a cup of tea. We all walked into the kitchen and Alice asked us to sit down at the table. Without saying a word, she made the tea. We just sat there feeling uncomfortable. Eventually, with tea and biscuits on the table, Alice asked me to start at the beginning and tell her once again about my meeting with her dad the day before. I ran through it all again, but this time she kept stopping me, asking me what he was wearing or how he looked. It was all very strange.

Eventually, I asked Alice if it was in her dad's power to sell the house and said that we would understand if he had acted without her consent. She nodded and said that the house used to be her dad's house but now it had passed to her. Then she dropped the bombshell: Doug had died from an unexpected heart attack three weeks ago. I gulped and nearly choked on my cup of tea. I assured Alice that I was not making any of this up and that I really had seen him yesterday. I even asked her if he had a twin. Alice was remarkably calm and coherent and told me that she believed me. My description of her dad was too accurate, especially what he had said about his garden. She also said that when he had died her Alice pen had been in his pocket but a few days afterwards it had gone missing.

Just at that moment the doorbell rang and she jumped up and told me that she had several viewings of the house scheduled for that day.

My wife looked at me with incomprehension as Alice left the room. I told her that I was not making anything up, but she was angry with me. 'You're telling me,' she said, rolling her eyes, 'that you spoke to the spirit of Alice's dad yesterday and he sold you the house? I'm sorry, Martin, but this really sounds too odd. Just you wait till the boys at the fire station here about this – you'll never hear the end of it.'

'I know it sounds odd,' said Alice, butting in. She must have overheard us from the hallway. 'But there is no doubt about it. Your husband saw my father in spirit and it's clear that he wants the two of you to live here. My dad said he would sort something out about the deposit, so I'll make sure that isn't a problem for you. I don't need a second home and I'm not living here. When do you want to move in?'

A week later we found out later why Alice was so sympathetic to our needs. Twenty years before, when she was just a child, she had been saved from a house fire by a fireman. He had risked his life to save hers and ever since that day she had believed in angels both in this life and the next.

We lived for ten happy years in Doug's home, eventually moving out when we had our third and fourth children. By then I'd been promoted at work and we could afford a bigger house. When it came to selling the house I made sure that it went to another young firefighter and his family struggling to get their feet on the property ladder. And every so often I still drop round to keep an eye on Doug's garden and to make sure it is being kept in the way that he would have wanted.

Until I met Doug I'd never really given the spiritual side of life much thought, but he changed my life in so many ways. As cynical as I used to be about life after death or angels, I now only see beautiful possibilities. I have no doubt that there is an afterlife. I've seen it with my own eyes.

Martin's story is remarkable in that it seems a house was sold to him by a spirit. Jennifer also had no idea at the time that she had met an angel.

Breakdown

We've all been there: it's late at night and your car breaks down in the middle of nowhere. I was travelling back from my friend's fortieth birthday party at a remote country pub when my car clattered to a halt. Luckily, there was enough life in it for me to get it safely to the side of the road.

Unluckily, there was not enough life left in my mobile phone for me to call for help.

I got out of my car to have a look around. It was so dark I could hardly see anything. I had a vague idea where I was, but I couldn't be sure. A couple of cars flashed past and I thought about asking one to stop but then I wondered if that was a good idea. The only other alternative was to wait until morning, but that was a good five hours away.

I sat back in my car and shivered with cold and with panic. The trees nearby looked really menacing and I shut my eyes in fear. And then I remembered someone I had met a few days ago back while I was filling my car with petrol. I'd been so panicked by the breakdown that it had slipped my mind. Anyway, a few days before I'd been at a petrol station. I'd just paid my bill and was heading back to my car when I noticed a petrol pump attendant standing by it and smiling. He didn't look weird or creepy, just friendly, so I was happy to smile back. He asked me if I had a long journey ahead and I told him I had. He said I should have something for my journey and put a manual mobile phone charger in my hand. I told him that I didn't have any cash on me but he insisted I take it and refused to take any payment. He told me that he worked for the garage and they were doing a promotion with the chargers. I was puzzled, but the man seemed so genuine and friendly that I decided to accept the charger.

So how daft was I? I had a mobile phone charger lying on the back seat of my car. I could use it now and get myself out of trouble. I plugged it in and started to wind and wind until my battery flickered into life. It didn't last long, but it was long enough to call the emergency pick-up services.

The next time I went to the garage to fill up I looked around for the attendant to thank him for getting me out of a sticky spot and to order some chargers for my friends. He was nowhere to be seen, so when I paid my bill I asked the cashier if they were still doing the manual phone-charger promotions. The woman clearly had no idea what I was talking about and neither did the manager, who was standing nearby. He told me that it was against company policy to do any promotions on the forecourt. So who was this guy? I'll never know for sure, but he was a guardian angel in my book.

Jennifer never saw the garage attendant again and she is convinced it was her guardian angel looking out for her.

Like Jennifer, Laura is also convinced that a guardian angel saved her from unexpected danger, this time when she was a schoolgirl.

Elle

I was 13 at the time and a bit of a tearaway. Normally, I'd have got the school bus home, but on that particular evening I stayed later than normal because I was in detention. Mum was working late but had given me money for a cab. I looked older than my age so I decided to buy cigarettes with the money instead and walk home through the park.

As I headed into the park it was about 5 p.m. and the light was starting to fail. The park was unusually empty and I hesitated for a moment but then I convinced myself I'd be fine. It was the wrong decision.

After a few minutes I noticed that a group of boys with hoods on was heading towards me. I thought about turning around and running but realized that would draw their attention to me, so I carried on. As I got closer to them I noticed that they were under the influence of alcohol or drugs. They were clearly not in control of their actions. It was getting quite dark now and the trees in the park obscured the light from the streets. I looked around, but there was nobody in sight. I forced myself to keep walking. It seemed as if it was the only thing I could do.

Suddenly a young woman stepped in front of me. I jumped in surprise, but she smiled at me and said reassuringly, 'There's safety in numbers. Just walk confidently.'

I noticed how good the woman's posture was and pushed my own shoulders back and my chin up. We walked straight towards the group of youths and they started to taunt and jeer at us. I began to feel very scared, but the woman told me to stay calm. I could see that one of the guys was carrying a metal bar, but the strangest thing happened when we walked towards him – he dropped it. Then the other youths stepped aside as if in a daze to let us walk through them. It was the weirdest sensation. They looked scared of us and as soon as we passed by they ran away.

When we had reached the other side of the park safely I thanked the woman. She told me that it might be a good idea to get a cab home in future if I was working late at school. It might also be a good idea to ditch the cigarettes, as they were a magnet for trouble. Finally, she told me that me that the decisions I made now would affect the rest of my life. I wondered how she could know all that about me but figured she was just a clued-up grown-up. Also, her words didn't really sink in at the time because I was so used to being lectured by adults.

That evening as I was watching the local news I saw her face flash up on the screen. I recognized her kind smile instantly. I could not believe my ears when I heard that her name was Elle and she had been killed in a hit and run accident that morning. I went to bed that night in a state of shock. Had I walked through the park that night with an angel?

The next day at school I was in trouble again. I wasn't concentrating in class. I was hauled into the headmistress's office and told that if my behaviour didn't turn around my mum and dad would be contacted. Suddenly, I remembered what Elle had said to me the night before about my actions now affecting the rest of my life. It was as if a light switched on inside me. If I wanted to have a decent life I needed to start taking responsibility for my actions. I needed to start playing by the rules.

After that, my headmistress credited my reformed character to her pep talk, but I know that it was Elle who had encouraged me to change the direction my life was heading in. I still wasn't the perfect pupil by any means, but after Elle saved my life in the park I stopped bunking off school, quit smoking and buckled down to work. I got a cluster of good grades and went on to teacher training college.

Twenty years on I've not told a soul this story, but every word of it is true. I do sometimes wonder if I should have reported my sighting to the police or even my headmistress, but looking back I still believe it was the right decision to stay quiet. I was just a child – a child with a reputation for getting into trouble – and they would never have taken me seriously.

Laura's dramatic story could be explained as a case of mistaken identity, but even if the woman who helped her wasn't a spirit, this doesn't explain the strange behaviour of the youths. Why were they so frightened of two unarmed women alone in a park? What stopped them from harming them?

And what stopped little Gemma and her big sister Jane from walking down a street?

Something in the Way

I was walking slowly down the street to my local shop for a newspaper one day with my little sister Gemma when she just stopped walking. I urged her on, but she seemed rooted to the spot. She was staring at something directly above her with her mouth wide open.

Suddenly there was a great crash – the wall in front of us had fallen down. Had we gone on I'm in no doubt that Gemma would have been crushed to death, as she was only three and far too small to have run away in time or survived the impact.

Shaking with the shock, I asked my sister why she had stopped.

'Didn't you see that huge, huge dinosaur with the long neck?' she said. 'He stood right in front of me and was so enormous I could not get past him.'

Gemma had never really spoken about dinosaurs before – I don't even think she knew what they were – but when I challenged her she insisted that this was exactly what she had seen.

When we got home I logged onto the internet to show her some dinosaur pictures and asked her to tell me which one she'd seen. I showed her lots of pictures and she eventually pointed to an Amygdalodon, a huge herbivorous creature up to 15 metres in length.

I know kids have an active imagination, but I'd never seen Gemma so spellbound before. Something I can't explain was blocking her way, and the more I think about it, the more I'm inclined to believe that it *was* a dinosaur. Imaginary or not, that dinosaur saved my sister's life and I'm eternally grateful for it.

The stories in this chapter show that people will see angels in the way they need to see them or the way that speaks loudest to them, even if that means a vision of a dinosaur! One person may see a burst of light in a darkened room or a full-blown angel complete with wings, another may see the cloudy form of someone they have lost, another may meet a mysterious stranger who guides them in the direction they need to be heading, yet another may sense a presence and get an instant feeling of well-being or love that lifts them emotionally rather than physically, and yet another person, like Sonia, who tells her story in her own words below, may actually feel themselves being carried in the gentle arms of an angel.

Carried in an Angel's Arms

About seven years ago I went horse riding with one of my oldest friends, Rebecca. She was an accomplished rider and passionate about horses. I loved horses, too, but didn't ride as regularly as Rebecca did.

I had a strange feeling as we drove to the stables that day, as if I knew something bad would happen, but Rebecca was so excited to be going riding with me that I didn't have the heart to tell her. She was going through a messy divorce at the time and I had booked this day for us both to help her take her mind off things.

When we arrived I explained to the stable owner that it had been a while since I'd been riding, so they gave me a quieter, older horse to ride. We were going on an hour-long trail and the first half-hour was great. It was a beautiful day and it made me feel good to see Rebecca look carefree and happy again. Then, as we approached the end of the trail, my 'quiet' horse bolted and there I was flying through the air. Then everything slowed right down and I felt as if I was being 'carried' to the ground. Rebecca later told me that it looked as if I was falling in slow motion. I felt myself being gently placed on the ground by soft arms. Then I heard the trainer rush over and things started to speed up again around me. The trainer checked me over and except for a bruise on my arm it was as though I hadn't fallen at all. Everybody was mystified. It turned out that my horse had bolted because it had scratched itself on barbed wire hidden by long grass. I should have fallen onto the wire fence, but it was as if I had been carried to the other side and laid on the grass. The trail leader said it was a miracle that I wasn't badly hurt.

I've tried to think of all sorts of logical explanations for it, but the only explanation I'm left with is that an angel carried me and saved me from being badly injured, even paralyzed. I feel truly blessed by the experience and am grateful for the opportunity to share it with a wider audience. I've talked about angels to a lot of people now and feel that this is what the angels want. The more we share angel stories and the more we believe in their power to help and comfort us in times of trouble, the more likely it is that miracles will happen.

Believing in angels and being open to an angelic experience brings an energy that makes it easier for angels to enter our lives, but, as these stories show, angels can appear in spontaneous and unexpected ways, whether a person believes in them or not. And however they choose to make their presence felt, there is one thing that every angel experience has in common: once an angel has touched a person's life things are never quite the same for them again. They discover a new sense of energy and purpose, a passionate belief in the afterlife that gives them the strength, conviction and courage to live the rest of their lives as they were meant to be lived – to the full.

Chapter 3

Earth Angels

I saw the tracks of angels in the earth,
The beauty of heaven walking by itself in the world.

Petrarch

How can you tell if an angel has stepped into your life? Sometimes you can't because angels often manifest as coincidences or in the guise of another person who is either consciously or unconsciously guided by a higher power. Later in this chapter we'll take a look at the divine work of these so-called 'Earth angels', but let's begin with coincidences or, as I sometimes call them, 'the work of angels done by people'.

Coincidences

Coincidences appear to be chance events, but to those who experience them they can often feel like part of a carefully orchestrated plan for their lives. Let's get something clear right from the start, though: angels will not run your life. No angel will interfere with your free will. Their function is not to do our work for us, but to help us to do it. If we can open our minds and hearts to them, they can guide us onto a path that will lead to happiness and hope. And one of their favourite ways to encourage us is through coincidences or synchronicity.

Have you ever been in a situation where you've been thinking about someone and then they've called or sent an e-mail? Or perhaps you've gone on holiday and met someone you went to school with? Or maybe a song has popped into your head and then minutes later you've heard it playing on the radio? Most of the time we forget about these kinds of coincidences, but coincidences are the language that angels speak and sometimes paying attention to a coincidence, even if it is a subtle one, can have a powerful life-changing effect. And every now and again it can have a truly universal effect. You're probably familiar with the story of Isaac Newton, the seven-teenth-century scientist who formulated the laws of gravity, but it is such a beautiful example of coincidence at work that I'd like you to bear with me and read about it one more time.

In junior school you may have heard how Newton made his great discovery about gravity not in a science lab but in the garden of his mother's home while on holiday. He went into the garden meditating on the 'why' questions of nature and as he sat there an apple fell from a nearby tree. Most people wouldn't have given it a second thought, but for Newton's questioning mind it was a moment of truth. He instantly understood that one of the laws of the universe is the attraction of mass to mass. It is this mutual attraction – the law of gravity – that keeps everything in the universe in its place.

Some conclude that Newton's theory suggests there is no higher power, but in my opinion the event that helped him formulate that theory was more than just coincidence. A higher force was involved. Angels wanted to open Newton's brilliant mind to how beautiful and orderly the world was – and to do this an apple was chosen, perhaps to counteract the disorder and sin that had marked the world when an earlier apple was plucked from a tree.

Certainly in my many years of collecting angel stories I have often marvelled at how apparently trivial events, like an apple falling from a tree or a lost object being found, can have an incredible effect. The coincidences that touched Ethan's life obviously can't match the universal effect of Newton's apple, but, as he explains below, from a personal point of view the impact was profound.

Going Home

I grew up in care. I never knew who my mother and father were. It was always just me and my sister. When I was 16 I left the children's home and two years later my sister did too. We both got married and had kids in our early twenties, but a few years later my sister went through a really messy divorce and decided to leave the country, taking her three young kids with her. She got a job teaching English as a foreign language in Spain and just packed her bags, took her kids and left. We exchanged Christmas and birthday cards for a few years, but then when she moved again, to Germany, and then again, to Italy, I lost touch with her. We'd been drifting apart for many years, so I wasn't that cut up about it. Besides, with three teenagers to support and my own business to run, I didn't have time for anything or anyone outside family or work.

We got close to it at times, but my wife and I never divorced. I think she knew that because of the struggles and turmoil I'd been through as a child I had problems with intimacy and trust, but we worked through them together and our relationship is stronger for it. As for my business, it thrived and although we weren't in the top 5 per cent of the country's earners, we were certainly very well off indeed by the time I celebrated my fiftieth birthday.

When my eldest son, Tom, left school he made it clear that he wasn't ready for work and that he wanted to see something of the world. I would have preferred him to help me out with the family business, but I realized that it was wrong to clip his wings when he was young. He needed to live a bit and do all the things I never had the opportunity to do when I was his age. So along with two of his best mates he set off on his adventure. I remember thinking as I waved him goodbye that it would have been good if he could have stayed with my sister for a while, but I had given up hope of ever finding her. I'd even started to believe that she didn't want to be found.

Every week or so in the next few months I would get an e-mail or a text or, if I was very lucky, a phone call from Tom. He was clearly having the time of his life, but then the communication stopped. A whole fortnight went by and I heard nothing. I tried his mobile and it was switched off. I was thinking about getting in touch with the police when the phone rang. My wife answered it and I could tell immediately by her screams of joy that it was Tom. The news got better. He was back in the UK and wanted us to pick him up from the airport. I asked about his two mates and he said they were continuing their adventures without him.

As we drove to the airport I wondered whether Tom was ready to settle down and get serious about his career now. I couldn't help but speculate as to why he had cut his

gap year short, but my wife made me promise not to inter-
rogate him for the first few days. There would be plenty of
time for that later.

When we arrived at the airport arrivals area we saw
Tom waiting with what looked like an emaciated boy, but
as we got closer I could see that he wasn't a boy, he was
a young man. Tom introduced me to Richard and then told
me something which winded me with surprise: this ill and
gaunt-looking individual was my nephew – my sister's
eldest son.

The airport was too busy to talk, so we welcomed
Richard and hugged Tom and then we all drove home.
Once we got home Tom told us that after Italy everyone
had decided to head for Holland. He apologized for not
letting me know but said there never seemed a right
moment, as he knew I would worry about him travelling
so extensively. To cut a long story short, while in Holland
he ending up checking into a dingy bed and breakfast for
the night. As he headed up the stairs to make his way to
his room he bumped into Richard, who offered to help him
carry his bag. Thinking he was working there, Tom gave
him the bag, but he regretted his decision immediately, as
Richard instantly hurtled down the stairs with it. He was
no match for Tom, though, who caught him before he had
even got to the bottom of the stairs.

The bed and breakfast owners asked Tom if he wanted
to press charges and were mighty relieved when he

spared their establishment the negative press and took pity on Richard, who was begging for forgiveness. To this day Tom, who has a strong sense of right and wrong, has no idea what on Earth compelled him not to report Richard to the police. He also has no idea why he felt strongly connected to the guy and so concerned for his well-being that instead of kicking him out on the street that day he offered to take him out for a good meal. Anyone who knows Tom knows that he isn't a soft touch, so this really was out of character.

It was during the meal that Tom discovered Richard wasn't a boy at all – he was actually 20 years old. He also found out that his mother had died 12 years before from a drugs overdose. Richard had no idea where his two sisters were, as after her death they had all been taken into different care homes. With no living relatives traced, he had been fostered by no fewer than five different couples, but nobody was willing to adopt him. From the age of 17 he had worked as a waiter, before spiralling downwards to a life of petty crime.

Hearing Richard's tragic story made Tom appreciate his happy childhood and loving upbringing more than ever and he started to think about returning home sooner rather than later. But he also felt an intense connection with Richard and knew that if he didn't offer to help him he might only have a few more years to live. And so for the next week Tom met Richard every day to make sure that he had a good meal.

When a certain degree of trust and friendship had been built up, Tom asked Richard if he would like to come and stay with him for a while in England. At first Richard wasn't sure about the idea. At 20 years old he was way beyond adoption, but Tom was persistent and a two-week stay was organized. It was only when arrangements for the flight home were made that the pieces of the puzzle began to fit together and Tom realized that the person he was taking home was his own cousin.

Although one of his sisters still can't be traced, Richard is now happily reunited with his other sister and working alongside Tom in the family business, but if you consider the chances of events turning out like this – the timing, the vast number of places in Holland Tom could have stayed, the huge number of people Richard could have attempted to steal a bag from – it's hard not to conclude that coincidences are the work of angels done by people.

The story of Richard and Tom is one of the strongest and most moving coincidence stories that I have ever read, but coincidences don't always have to be so powerful to transform lives. In fact when you think about the significant people in your life right now, hasn't coincidence played a huge part? Take your partner or your closest friends, for example. Life would-n't make sense without them, but think about how acci-dental your first meeting probably was. If you had not gone to a particular school, college, party, meeting or lecture, if you had not walked down a certain street or stepped into a shop or taken a train on one particular day, you might never have met. The chance involved in the beginnings of friendship suggests that there is a higher power bringing the significant people in your life to you. As Isabelle's story illustrates, if seen in this light, there is no such thing as two people or a group of people who are happy together – there is always a higher force between them.

Friends Reunited

I was at a café in one of London's busy neighbourhoods enjoying a latte at a table overlooking the street when a woman asked if she could take one of the empty chairs by my table. I was happy to oblige. Unfortunately for her, as she was dragging the chair across to her table the edge of her coat knocked over her latte, and milk and froth gushed all over the floor. My first reaction was to gasp in sympathy, but then I looked at her and we both started giggling.

This was like *déjà vu*. We had both been in this situa-tion before. In fact I knew this woman. She had been my best friend at junior school and our friendship had begun over a bottle of spilled milk.

When I was going to school it was still compulsory to drink a half-pint of milk at morning break time. 'Thatcher the milk snatcher' took that away, but not soon enough for me. I love the taste of milk, but for some reason the milk at school always tasted slightly sour. I dreaded drinking it and would try every trick on the book to avoid it. There was also a girl in my class called Monica. She had curly black hair which was tied in bunches. She was a bit of a comedian and I envied her ease with people. I wanted to be her friend but I was painfully shy and didn't know how to approach her, as she seemed so popular. Then one morning during milk break Monica winked at me and then deliberately dropped her milk bottle so that it smashed all over the place. The teacher, whose back was turned at the time, demanded to know what happened and then turned to me to ask if it was dropped deliberately or accidentally. I was a bit of a Goodie Two Shoes at school, so the teacher knew I was probably the child most likely to tell the truth. Normally I would have, but I wanted to be Monica's friend and I told my teacher it had been an accident. Monica and I were best friends from that moment onwards until we went our separate ways at secondary school.

In the café there was so much to catch up on and we talked for hours. We made a resolve never to lose touch again and we have both been true to our word. The coincidence doesn't stop there, though, because there was one person we were both eager to talk about. It was a girl in our class we both liked called Pauline who eventually became head girl and made us both prefects. And would you believe it, at the precise moment that we were talking about her, who should come up to us and introduce herself but Pauline herself! She had overheard us talking about her as she had been ordering a cappuccino. Now was that a coincidence or was that a coincidence?

Clearly Isabelle's story is a brilliant coincidence, but in my mind it is also says a great deal about the power of true friendship. Monica and Isabelle could have visited any number of cafés that day and even if they had visited the same one on the same day, without the spilt milk incident they might never have recognized each other. And what was it that made Pauline walk in just as they were talking about her?

Ring of Truth

Here's another coincidence story that is simply astonishing. When I first read Barbara's story, written in her own words below, there were tears in my eyes.

Ian and I were sweethearts at school and as soon as we left school we got engaged. We wanted to get married as soon as possible but postponed the wedding because of the war. The next five years were tough – very tough indeed – and my heart fluttered every time the doorbell rang or the post arrived. We wrote to each other as much as we could and I tried to get on with my life, but it was torture being apart. I still have every one of Ian's letters and he kept every one of mine. To take his mind off things, in my letters I talked a lot about our wedding and he talked a lot about the ring he wanted to buy me. He told me he wanted me to have the most beautiful wedding band ever and he wanted it to be engraved.

So many of my friends lost their sweethearts when they were posted overseas, but by the mercy of God, Ian came back safely to me. We didn't get married straight away, as we needed to save some money, but after a few years the day I had been waiting so long for arrived. It was every bit as beautiful as I had wished and the wedding ring Ian gave me was incredible. To this day I have no idea how he managed to afford it. It was beautifully designed and at least half an inch wide, and engraved on it were the words 'Our love is true and forever', with our wedding date, 9/6/50.

We went to Scotland for three weeks for our honeymoon and every second was magic. On the last evening we went out for one more romantic meal by the lakeside.

Feeling a little stuffed, we decided to walk along the lake and, it being our honeymoon, we also decided to have a cuddle on the shore. Eventually, we headed back to the hotel and I started to get ready for bed. It was then that I realized my wedding ring was gone. Frantically, we searched everywhere in the hotel room. We phoned the restaurant the next morning and retraced our steps along the lake, but there was no sign of the ring. You can imagine how upset I was, especially as Ian had talked about the ring so much and saved up so hard to buy it.

We did all we could, but eventually we had to admit defeat – the ring was gone. On the way back home in the coach I found it hard to fight back the tears. Ian comforted me as best he could and told me that I didn't need a ring to know how much he loved me. Rings were easy to buy but our love and companionship weren't.

A few months later Ian bought me an equally gorgeous ring and although I was very happy with it I never told him that I always yearned for the first one.

Twenty years and three kids later I was as much in love with Ian as I had ever been. Life was good and the children a constant source of delight, but my happiness was to be shattered when on 1 June 1972 Ian was killed in a car accident. I was told that he had died instantly and that he hadn't suffered, but the pain was unbearable. Almost all my life Ian had been in my thoughts and in my heart and I had no idea how I would cope without him. Of course I had to be strong with the kids, but when I was alone the tears never stopped flowing. I begged him to send me a sign that he was still with me.

I decided to scatter Ian's ashes in Scotland, as we had both been so happy there on our honeymoon. When we arrived, Ian's sister had organized a light fish supper for us at a restaurant with a fine reputation that had recently opened. I found it hard to eat, but I forced a morsel or two into my mouth. Perhaps I didn't chew my food properly before swallowing, or perhaps my throat was really dry because of all the crying, but I started to choke on something, probably a fish bone. I couldn't breathe, but mercifully the feeling passed and I was able to swallow. By then the manager had rushed to my side, ready to administer first aid, and he was mighty relieved to see that I was OK. I was relieved, too, as nearly choking to death reminded me how much I had to live for – my children and my grandchildren needed me.

With the incident over, a kind-looking waitress about the same age as me asked me if I was OK. I nodded and said that it was more the shock and the embarrassment now. She smiled at me and told me that a few years back her husband had nearly choked on an ear-ring that had somehow made its way into a fish's stomach. It had been a really scary couple of minutes. 'Fish end up eating the strangest things,' she went on to say. 'I've even heard stories of people choking on buttons and rings found in fish's stomachs.' As soon as she mentioned rings I thought about my long-lost wedding ring and wondered out loud if a fish had eaten that all those years ago.

You could have knocked me over with a feather when I heard the waitress tell me that about 20 years ago she had found a wedding ring when she was out walking her dog along the lakeshore one morning. She had seen the dog scratching in the sand and then putting something in his mouth and hadn't been able to believe her eyes when he had spat out a gold wedding ring. Shakily, I asked her if the ring was engraved with the words 'Our love is true and forever' and she nodded. Then I told her that the wedding ring was mine and I had lost it on my honeymoon.

The waitress was only too happy to return the ring to me. She had been tempted to sell it on many occasions but for some reason she couldn't explain had decided to keep it all those years. She told me she had even placed an advertisement in the local newspaper, but no one who had tried to claim it had known the words engraved on it, so she knew they were frauds.

Later that night I stood on the very lakeshore where I had lost my ring all those years ago. Now it had found its way back to its true owner and was glittering on my hand in the moonlight. You can call it a series of strange coincidences if you like, but for me it was proof that my beloved Ian was watching over me.

Not surprisingly Barbara has never let her lost-and-found ring out of her sight since. It is a constant reminder that in this life and the next the love between her and Ian is true and forever.

I'd like to round up this section on coincidences with a couple of stories that show that angels do have a lighter side. If you have ever wondered whether angels know how to laugh, Mary's unforeseen circumstance story shows that they certainly do.

Wedding Ringers

My sister Jacky has always been a perfectionist and when she eventually decided to get married to her boyfriend Dave, I knew that the wedding preparations were going to be an ordeal. We had our differences but I loved my sister, so I did everything she wanted and spent hours and days and weeks and months listening to her talking about wedding venues, invitations, cakes and so on. She took ages to decide who was respectable enough to invite. Only the very best would do. I also ended up wearing the bridesmaid's dress of her choice. It was ridiculously frilly and made of nylon, but I wanted my sister to have what she wanted on her wedding day.

Anyway, on the wedding day itself the church was covered tastefully with flowers and baskets and ribbons. As Jacky walked up the aisle on Dad's arm she looked beautiful, but as I looked at the bride's face and groom's face and the faces of the hundreds of guests I couldn't help but think that there was one important thing missing – nobody was smiling. This was supposed to be the happiest day of my sister's life and she looked tense. I longed to see her smile.

When she reached the altar everyone sat down and the solemn vows began. Suddenly, loud and clear in the silence of the church, a mobile phone rang, with the ringtone set to perhaps the most unsuitable song for a wedding ever, 'Crazy Frog'. About five or so people reached into their pockets or bags to check it wasn't their mobile going off – proving in an instant to my sister that they all had terrible taste in music – but the culprit turned out to be the priest himself, who apologized profusely for forgetting to turn his phone off. My sister looked cross, but then she started giggling and before long everyone was howling with laughter – just the way it should be at a wedding, in my opinion.

By a strange coincidence Mary's wish to see her sister smile on what should have been the happiest day of her life was granted by the vicar's unusual choice of ringtone. And like Mary, Diana also discovered that as far as angels are concerned, seriousness of purpose and a light touch can go hand in hand ...

Falling Apart

It's been five years since my husband died and I still haven't got used to taking care of myself. I'm helpless when it comes to DIY or gardening. My son helps out as much as he can, but I don't like to bother him. Anyway, one day I decided that I needed to dismantle a small shed in our garden that had been there for years serving no purpose. I wanted the land to grow some of my own vegetables.

After removing everything inside the shed, I tried to take out some of the screws holding everything together. It was impossible, as they had been screwed in so tightly by my husband's strong hands. It was incredibly frustrating and exhausting and I only managed to remove one piece of the roof. I realized there was no way I was going to be able to do this myself. Feeling pathetic and helpless, I started to cry, as it was at times like these that I missed my husband more than ever.

Then suddenly, before my very eyes, the shed just *fell apart*. I could not believe it. I hadn't even asked the angels to help me. When the dust settled, all I had to do was pick everything up and clear it away.

My shed inexplicably and unexpectedly falling down is proof to me that angels can help even when we don't really need their assistance. And I'm still amazed that they aren't so serious or high and mighty that they are above taking a garden shed apart.

Angels on Earth

Coincidences are a common example of times when we can get glimpses of the angels at work right here on Earth, but angels can also manifest their loving presence through people.

In the previous chapter we saw a couple of examples of angels working their magic through the actions of people. Regardless of whether or not these people realize they are being guided by a higher power, I like to call them 'Earth angels'. In Lauren's mind there is no doubt that an Earth angel saved her life.

'Can I Have the Bill Please?'

It had been a busy shopping morning with Mum and we decided to treat ourselves to lunch. We had a lovely meal, although it was slightly spoiled by a woman on the table opposite. She had two young children with her and they were very noisy. At one point I nearly went over to her and asked her to keep her children quiet, but my mum stopped me and gently reminded me that when I was their age I was just as noisy. Being only 17 at the time, I told her with all the arrogance of youth that when I became a mother I would make sure I kept my children quiet in public and if they couldn't stay quiet I would keep them at home. My mother shrugged her shoulders and smiled at me.

After we had eaten our main course the waitress asked if we wanted dessert. Mum was about to order a chocolate cake but I stopped her and requested the bill instead. When Mum asked why, I told her that the kids on the table opposite were just too noisy and I'd buy her a cake or something on the way home. The bill arrived and Mum reached for her purse to pay. There were a couple of mints with the bill, so I popped one into my mouth. It tasted delicious and I spent a few moments savouring the cool freshness.

As we sorted out our credit card payment my mum started to talk to me about the nervous sales assistant we had encountered on our morning shop. This woman must have asked us at least four times if we were alright or needed any help. Her hovering presence had got so annoying that we'd decided we couldn't stay in the shop a moment longer and when she'd been momentarily distracted from tail-gating us, we'd bolted out. I started to giggle as I remembered the incident, but as I did so my mint got stuck in my throat.

I can't recall much about it, as I think I was close to passing out. My mum tells me it was one of the most frightening moments of her life. All I can remember is that I was fighting to breathe and every second seemed like an eternity. Then all of a sudden the woman sitting next to us shot forward, grabbed me from behind with both arms and lifted me up. Later I was to learn that she had performed what is called the Heimlich manoeuvre and this dislodged my mint instantly. This woman with the two noisy children saved my life.

My mum held me close, sobbing, and when I got my breath back I looked around to thank the woman, but there was no sign of her or her children. Even more curious was that her table was clear and the waitress had no recollection of her. I went on my local radio station to ask if she could come forward, but she never did.

I shall never forget that woman. Ten years later, with two of my own very noisy kids, both at home and in public I hasten to add, I think about her a lot. Without her I might not have become a mother at all. Was she my guardian angel waiting in the restaurant for the moment when she knew I was going to choke on my after-dinner mint? Or was she a kind Samaritan with first aid skills? It doesn't really matter at the end of the day, because either way she was heaven sent for me.

Was the woman who saved Lauren an angel? It's up to you, but I've read and heard enough Earth angel stories over the years to be convinced that angels do often watch over us and sometimes save our lives in the guise of other people. I am also convinced that sometimes they place people in our lives to give us encouragement, love, skills and hope at just the time we need it or when we feel everything in our life is going wrong. Mark believes that as a young man he met an Earth angel who gave him the hope and faith he needed to get through a family tragedy:

The Fifth Floor

When you are 16 and the only loving parent you have known is your grandfather, hearing that your grandfather may die shatters your world into pieces. My mother died from breast cancer when I was four and then my dad did a runner, leaving my grandfather to take care of me. As I was growing up I knew a lot of my mates felt sorry for me because I didn't have any parents, but because I had never really got to know either of my parents I never really missed them much. Besides, my grandfather was such a character. He had more energy than any of the other parents put together. Before becoming a theatre agent he had worked as a professional magician and he made sure that my childhood was as magical as possible. My upbringing may have been unconventional, but I don't think I can remember a day when my grandfather and I didn't laugh together or do fun, exciting things. He was my mother and my father – my entire family – and I would have gone to the ends of the Earth for him.

A week after my seventeenth birthday I got a message at school telling me that my grandfather had suddenly been taken ill and had been rushed to hospital. My teacher drove me to the hospital and told me that my grandfather was on the fourth floor and that I should call her if I needed anything or a lift back home. With a heavy heart I watched her car disappear. A part of me wished that she had stayed. This was really tough to cope with alone, but then I thought about what a fighter my grandfather was and convinced myself that however ill he was he would pull through.

I took the lift to the fourth floor and when I arrived a nurse directed me to my grandfather's room. Crumpled sheets and heavy-looking pillows seemed to be covering him completely. I gazed at his tired face. It was drawn and motionless. His eyes were closed and for the first time I noticed how many wrinkles he had. He looked old and pale. I reached for his hand and held it tight, but his fingers felt limp and cold. Then I noticed all the tubing running from his chest and arms to drips by his bed. 'This isn't Grandfather,' I remember thinking. The beep of his heart monitor echoed harshly in my ears. What had happened to the grandfather I remembered? He had always been there for me. When I was little he would take me to school and pick me up with arms outstretched every day and when I got older it felt so good to come home to his smiling face.

A doctor came into the room and introduced himself. He asked me if there was anyone I could call and I told him that it was just me and my grandfather. He then started to tell me that my grandfather had had a heart attack and that his condition was serious. He used a lot of technical terms that I can't remember because the only words that sunk in were 'Not sure if he will make it.'

Filled with despair, I sat down by my grandfather and begged him to wake up. There was so much I wanted to tell him. The doctor shook his head and told me that my grandfather was unconscious now and couldn't hear me. He told me that the best thing I could do was go home and get some rest.

When the doctor left I felt my eyes stinging with tears. I looked at my grandfather again and mixed with my grief I felt frustration and anger. I wanted to speak to him but he didn't even know I was there. I might as well *not* be there. How could he do this to me? Who was going to be there for me? I grabbed my bag and all I could think about was getting out of the hospital and never going back.

'It's OK to feel angry,' a voice behind me said. I turned around and saw a man about the same height as me. He had blond hair and blue eyes and the whitest teeth I'd ever seen. He looked like a doctor, as he was carrying a clipboard and had a white coat on. 'And let me assure you,' he continued, 'your grandfather does know you are here.'

It was as if this guy was reading my mind.

'You're probably wondering who I am,' he said gently. 'I work on the fifth floor and if your grandfather gets well enough – which I think he might – that is where they will move him to recover.'

'I feel so useless,' I replied. 'And how can you tell he knows I'm here?'

The man smiled and said, 'Experience. You being here is the most important thing in the world right now for your grandfather. He can hear every word you say. Keep talking to him. He needs to hear you.'

Suddenly, I didn't feel so helpless anymore. I felt that I was needed. I don't know why, but there was something about this man that made me believe every word he said. He squeezed my shoulder and said he had to get back to work, but if I needed anyone to talk to he would be on the fifth floor. I thanked him and sat down by my grandfather's bed again. I held his hand as tightly as I could and started to talk about my day at school, my friends, what I wanted to eat for tea – anything that came to my mind. I even told him about a few bad grades I'd got recently in my Biology A-level mock. I must have chatted to him for three or four hours before tiredness got the better of me and I nodded off.

When I woke up it was well into the evening and grandfather was still lying motionless in his bed. I stretched and went outside to grab a soda and something to eat. When I got back I couldn't believe my eyes – my grandfather had his eyes open. I dashed over to him and asked him how he was feeling. 'A little tired and sore,' he replied, 'but so much better than when you came to see me this morning.' And then he winked, pretending to frown, and said, 'But we need to sort out those Biology grades.'

The gentle man had been right – my grandfather had been aware that I had been with him all day. He had heard everything but had just been too exhausted to respond. And, again just as the man had said, when the nurses and doctor had checked him over he was moved to the fifth floor – the recovery floor.

I do sometimes wonder if my grandfather would have pulled through if the man hadn't encouraged me to stay with him. I also wonder if the man was an angel, as I looked everywhere for him on the fifth floor and never found him – or anyone matching his description.

That experience was just the beginning for me – the beginning of a life-long belief in angels, both human and divine. And in my heart that day I understood how loving words can work miracles.

Mark's grandfather lived for another seven years and when he eventually died Mark told me that his Earth angel experience at the hospital helped him to cope better with the loss. He knows that his grandfather will never stop listening to him and being there for him in the afterlife, just as he always was in this life.

Anna's story is similar to Mark's in that it also demonstrates the awesome power of a few well-chosen words at a moment of crisis:

Don't Know What to Say

When you are 21 years old with the world waiting for you to discover it, you never pause for one moment to think that you could lose it all in a split-second. I was in my final year of university and I couldn't wait to get out in the world and make my mark. Ever since I was about five years old I'd wanted to be a pilot. My mum and sister supported me but I could always tell they were worried about accidents. I tried to reassure them by saying that there was far more chance of having an accident in your car or in your home than in an aeroplane. My words would return to haunt me.

I'd been to a party and had had a little too much to drink. I knew I was over the limit but I also prided myself on being a sensible and safe driver, so I decided to drive myself home. I must have dozed off at the wheel, though, because the next thing I can remember is being in hospital. Apparently I'd collided with a truck and crashed into a tree. The truck driver mercifully didn't have any injuries, but I had enough for the both of us — which I suppose you could say was just, because the accident was entirely my fault.

So there I was in hospital with a broken spine. Doctors told me it was unlikely I would ever walk again. One stupid, stupid decision and my life had changed forever, my dreams of becoming a pilot – of becoming anything – left behind in my shattered car.

For the first few weeks I was numb with shock and the reality of it didn't sink in. But then about a month after my accident it hit me like a sledgehammer hitting a bruise over and over again: *I wasn't ever going to walk again.*

One of the worst things was that my family and friends just didn't know what to say to me. What could anyone say? Nothing anyone said or did could make this go away.

Needless to say, a part of me wished I had died in the accident. I had no appetite. I couldn't sleep. I felt that my life was over and if I could have got my hands on lots of sleeping pills I would willingly have taken them. I had no interest in seeing my friends and eventually their visits tapered off. I'm not surprised, because when they came I would just turn away from them. I gave my family an even harder time, especially my mother, as I cursed the day I was born. All I wanted was to be left alone.

My depression lasted for several months. An endless round of specialists and therapists came to see me, but none of them made me feel any better. There wasn't anything I wanted to live for. I wanted to die.

Then one morning a lady came into my room. She had a smart blue suit on and a bunch of flowers in her hand. I assumed she was another therapist and told her that I didn't want any flowers and that there was no point bringing them because they would wither and die anyway.

The woman snorted and replied, 'These beautiful flowers, they aren't for you anyway. I'm here visiting my sister. She loves getting flowers. Why on Earth would I want to give you flowers if that's the way you talk to people?'

This woman was the first person since my accident to be rude to me. Everyone else had been so terribly earnest and kind, but this woman was talking to me as if I was normal. Her frankness sparked my interest.

'I've got every right to talk that way,' I replied. 'I've lost the use of my legs.'

'That doesn't give you the right to be rude,' she answered. 'My sister has lost her leg and she is the sweetest, kindest angel and only 14 years old.'

The woman's eyes went moist as she mentioned her sister and suddenly I felt a wave of sympathy for her misfortune.

'I'm sorry,' I whispered. 'How is she coping?'

'Better than you, I think.'

When I heard that, I started to cry. I literally fell apart.

I have never cried so hard in my life.

The woman came over to me and held me gently. 'You know,' she said, staring intently at me, 'your angel won't give you anything that you can't handle.'

Suddenly, I felt as if a massive weight had been lifted off my shoulders. I didn't feel alone anymore. The woman gave me a reassuring smile then left. Her words came to me when I was in the depths of despair and I have never forgotten them. They were the turning point in my life.

Today, I am happily married with a beautiful daughter. I run my own model aircraft business and am a keen swimmer. I never got to fly in the physical sense, but there isn't a day that goes by that my spirit doesn't soar in the spiritual sense. I truly believe that the woman in the hospital, even though I don't know her name, was an angel sent to me when I needed her most.

Angels can choose to appear in their traditional form, complete with wings and halo, but far more common and just as uplifting and positive are angels who manifest in human form. I think the following poem, by an unknown author, says it far better than I can:

What Do Angels Look Like?

Like the little old lady who returned
your wallet yesterday.
Like the taxi driver who told you that your eyes
light up the world when you smile.
Like the small child who showed you
the wonder in simple things.
Like the poor man who offered to
share his lunch with you.
Like the rich man who showed you that it
really is all possible, if only you believe.
Like the stranger who just happened to come along
when you had lost your way.
Like the friend who touched your heart
when you didn't think you had one to touch.
Angels come in all sizes and shapes,
all ages and skin types and colours.
Some with freckles, some with dimples,
some with wrinkles, some without.
They come disguised as friends, enemies,
nurses, teachers, students, lovers and fools.
They don't take life too seriously.
They travel light.
They leave no forwarding address.
They ask nothing in return.
They wear sneakers with gossamer wings.

They get a deal on dry cleaning.
They are hard to find when your eyes are closed,
but they are everywhere you look,
when you choose to open your eyes and see.

Yes, Earth angels come in all colours, sizes and ages. Although they don't always arrive with a blast of trumpets, or have feathered wings or halos, they are angels just the same. Some Earth angels mysteriously disappear and are impossible to trace, while others borrow the faces of family, friends or passing strangers, who may or may not be aware that angels are guiding them. Anyone who raises your spirits or helps you to grow or love is an angel and at this point in the book I think you might enjoy this story sent to me by Natalie:

Angel at the Petrol Pump

I had the most incredible experience and I want to share it with you. It happened six months ago, a week before Christmas. I was driving home and looking forward to a night in as I'd done a lot of trips for work recently and was thinking it would be good to have some 'me' time. But then I got stuck in an endless traffic jam and my car began to splutter and make strange noises. I started to get really worried when the driver behind me hooted and pointed to my exhaust and the dirt and smoke it was coughing out.

Cursing my misfortune, I coasted to the nearest petrol station. I didn't want to block the traffic and I needed somewhere safe to see what was happening underneath my car. As soon as I arrived my car just packed up, so I literally rolled into the forecourt and parked it out of harm's way. I tried the ignition several times, but the car was dead.

I got out of the car and took a look underneath. Everything looked perfectly fine so I got in again and tried the ignition, but once again there was nothing, just a whirring sound. I was just about to make a call to the RAC when I saw a young woman with two toddlers coming out of the petrol station. It was a cold night and she caught my attention because she didn't have a coat on. She looked freezing. I watched her bend down to button up her children's coats and then as she got up she grabbed her back and yelled in pain. I've suffered from backache myself and I know it is excruciating, so I really felt for her as she started to limp away with her children tugging at her. She only managed a few steps and had to rest against a petrol pump. With time on my hands, I decided to get out of my car to check she was OK.

When I got to her I could see that she was much younger than I'd thought – barely out of her teens. She also had huge dark circles under her eyes. I could tell she was fighting back tears. When I asked her if she was OK, all she could say was, 'I can't let the kids see me cry.' She then took a deep breath and went on to explain that she was driving to stay at her sister's place. Life was really tough for her right now. She had left her partner because he drank too much and she was worried he would hurt her kids. She hadn't spoken to her sister for two years but she had said she could stay with her while she got back on her feet.

As the girl was speaking I looked at her shivering in the cold and thought about my warm coat in the car and how the warmth would really be good for her back. The coat was a gift from my mum but I had several other coats and didn't really need it, so I rushed back to my car and gave it to her. At first she didn't want to accept it, but I told her she was doing me a favour because I didn't want it anymore. It was good to see her face look a little less pale when she put it on. I think the warmth of the coat also eased her back pain, as she stood up straight then. The children began tugging on the coat, asking for something to eat, but the girl shook her head. It became clear to me then that she didn't have enough money to buy them any food, so without hesitation I took her inside the garage shop and bought fruit, crisps, sandwiches and other snacks. She gave the food to her children and they attacked it like wolves.

All the while the girl couldn't stop thanking me. I started to feel a little embarrassed, as I'm not normally the kind of person who does this kind of thing. I prefer to help others by writing a cheque or donating to a charity and being this direct wasn't my style. However, something was urging me on and I knew deep down inside I was doing the right thing. I had a couple of painkillers in my bag so I gave them to the girl for her backache and helped her get back to her car. Once she was inside I gave her my gloves and a £50 note and wished her well. She thanked me again and as I started to walk away, she shouted after me, 'So, are you like a Christmas angel or something? I've read stories about people like you.'

This time it was my turn to cry. I turned around and what I said next just tumbled out of my mouth: 'Christmas is a really busy time for angels, so sometimes regular people like me need to give them a helping hand.'

There have been times in my life when I've felt happy – like when I got my first pay cheque or when my boyfriend first asked me out or when I managed to finally fit into a size 12 pair of jeans – but nothing can compare to the feeling I had that night as I watched that girl drive away smiling and waving at me. It was incredible to be a part of someone's miracle and to be able to touch someone's life in a practical way.

And, of course, you guessed it, when I got back to my car there was nothing wrong with it. I gave the ignition one last try and to my surprise it was working perfectly. I checked the exhaust and there was no dirt and dust spitting out. My car got me home with no problem and when I took it into the garage for a service the next day the mechanic didn't find anything wrong, which makes me think that I was meant to stop at that petrol station so that I could give that girl – I don't even know her name – the warmth, support and hope she so urgently needed.

This story reminds us that it isn't just other people who do heavenly work – angels can exist within each one of us. In fact one of the most powerful ways to connect with angels is to discover them from the inside out. Many of us don't realize that everything we do and say has the potential to touch others in a heavenly way. Whenever you feel love or compassion for someone you are being an angel. A single happy smile can brighten someone's day, a kind and gentle word can help someone find beauty in their life and a tiny act of kindness can create a ray of sunshine in the lives of others. I can think of no better way to conclude this Earth angel chapter than with this short but perfect story:

On the street I saw a little boy cold and shivering in a thin pair of shorts and a threadbare shirt. I became angry and asked the angels, 'Why did you permit this? Why don't you do something about it?'

My guardian angel replied, 'I certainly did do something about it – I brought you here.'

Chapter 4

Angels, Spirits and Signs

Every raindrop that falls is accompanied by an Angel.
For even a raindrop is a manifestation of being.

The Prophet Mohammad

Spirits of lost loved ones are not angels in the traditional
sense of the word, but in this book I call them angels
because angels often manifest their message of loving
guidance and support through the spirit of a lost loved
one.

If you have ever lost a loved one you'll know that
mixed with a sense of loss, grief, loneliness, confusion
and emptiness there can sometimes be a hint of anger or
resentment at the harsh injustice of the world. Why has
this happened to me? Why now? There may also be feelings of anger towards the lost loved one. When my
mother died, a part of me was furious. I felt abandoned.
How could she do this to me? How could she leave me
now, when I needed her so much?

The loss of a loved one is one of the hardest things anyone will ever have to face emotionally. But time and time again I've seen how this challenging and complex emotional journey becomes so much easier to bear when the person who is grieving receives a sign which helps them understand that death is not the end but a brilliant new beginning.

For me the sign that finally released my feelings of resentment, hurt and tension was the cloud in the perfect shape of an angel, but there are countless ways for loved ones to come back to us to prove that they have not abandoned us. In the last ten years I've collected thousands of stories from ordinary people who have experienced unique signs from departed loved ones. These signs range from distinctive aromas to kettles switching on spontaneously and withered plants flowering, but whatever they are, they all have one thing in common: they provide those who are grieving with joy and comfort. They offer proof that there is no such thing as death, only a transition to the world of spirit. This is Peter's experience of an angel sign:

Picture Perfect

My wife was beautiful – the stop and stare in the street kind of beautiful. If I had had a pound for every time someone else said, 'What on Earth does she see in you?' I'd be a wealthy man indeed.

We'd been married for a happy four years when she died. She went into hospital for a routine gynaecological procedure but this led to a diagnosis of ovarian cancer. I don't want to go into the details, but I can tell you the last year of her life was an ordeal physically and emotionally. To the last her concern was always for me and the children.

After the funeral I found myself alone with my two little boys, perhaps for the first time. You see, until her diagnosis my wife had been the main carer and when she got ill my sister had stepped into look after the boys. The first few months were ghastly and I can't really remember much. I knew I needed to spend time with the kids, but looking at them reminded me of my wife. I hired a nanny, but she wasn't right for the job, so I decided to send my boys to nursery. This wasn't ideal, but they seemed to settle better. As for me, I buried myself in work. My sister would collect the boys from nursery and give them tea; often I'd not be home until they were tucked up in bed.

Weekends were the biggest strain. I'd spend hours cleaning and tidying the house and when I wasn't doing housework I would retire to my study to catch up on work. We all have different ways of coping with loss and, looking back, the way I chose to cope was to become a workaholic. I also became quite obsessive about cleanliness. I wanted my house to look perfect, just as my wife had left it before she died. My sons got used to Daddy being busy with work or too tired to play.

I had to appear strong, but there were times when I didn't feel strong at all. I don't know how I would have coped without my sister. She was the only one who actually saw me cry. She was the only one I could tell how lonely I was feeling.

One Saturday when she dropped round for a chat I was feeling particularly low. I was exhausted and the house was untidy. There were kids' toys everywhere. I desperately needed a break from the house and the kids, but in my mind this was impossible. My sister offered to take the kids for a week, but I felt as though I would be betraying my wife if she did. You see, in the last few days before her death she had made me promise that I would always put the boys first and be both their mother and their father. I felt ashamed because I clearly wasn't up to the task.

My sister held my hand and told me that I needed a break. 'I think you need some time out. You can't go on like this. Something has got to give.' I wasn't so sure and told her there was so much I needed to do at work. And then my sister hit me where it hurt. 'If you want the honest truth,' she said, taking a deep breath, 'I don't think your kids would know you'd gone, as you hardly ever see them anyway.'

'That's not true,' I said, but in my heart I knew my sister was telling the truth. I started to unload the dishwasher, hoping to distract myself from the pain I felt inside. How I wished I could talk things through with my wife. I didn't know what to do. Would my wife have wanted me to go?

At that point, a picture of my wife in the kitchen suddenly fell down and clattered to the floor. Little pieces of glass went everywhere.

'There's your answer,' my sister said.

I picked up the picture and brushed the broken glass away from my wife's smiling face. I studied it for a while and it gave me strength. Then I noticed something I'd never noticed before. In the picture she was sitting at her desk and her hand was resting on a book. The title of the book was *Don't Sweat the Small Stuff*. I have no doubt that my wife was trying to tell me something important.

A week later I did go on holiday, but I took the boys with me. The picture falling to the floor was the shock I'd needed – a timely reminder from the world of spirit that life is far too short and that nobody on their deathbed wishes they had spent more time in the office or cleaning the house. What mattered was spending time with my children.

Being away together did us all the world of good and when I came back the house was as untidy as I had left it and the answerphone was flashing with messages. But instead of immediately unpacking, opening post, whizzing around with a duster or returning calls, the first thing I did was order a takeaway and chase around the garden with my kids.

Peter's story shows that the spirits of loved ones don't want to see us tortured by grief or living a life that is limited; they want to see us living our lives to the full. The picture of his wife falling at just the moment when Peter was trying to decide what to do was the sign that he needed to help him understand that his wife wasn't far away and that she needed him to become the father she always knew he could be.

Dawn's story is another fine example of how noticing and then understanding the sign of an angel can open a person's mind and heart:

Living Doll

My best Christmas present ever – and I've had some good ones over the years – was an heirloom doll. My gran gave it to me when I was eight and not only did the doll have my blonde hair and brown eyes, but my gran had gone to the trouble of making a whole wardrobe of clothes for it that were an exact copy of mine. There was a cord on the back of the doll and when you pulled it

'Somewhere over the Rainbow' played with gentle chimes. I had just played the part of Dorothy in my school production, so I couldn't have been happier with my present. The cord broke after a few months, so the music didn't play anymore. We took it to a toy maker but they said that repairing it was impossible because they would have to take the doll apart. The real magic for me was dressing the doll up in the wonderful clothes Gran had made, so I just accepted that it wouldn't play my song anymore.

The junior school years were my golden years, when I look back. I got the main part in the school play and good grades and in the final year was even asked to be head girl. My parents had high expectations for me – perhaps too high! When I became a teenager, I started to rebel. I stopped caring about school and hung around with the wrong crowd. I dropped out of the school musical theatre club and went through a rough time with my parents. At one point the situation was so bad that I packed my bags and moved in with my gran. She never criticized and just accepted me for who I was. I ended up staying with her for almost a year. Things were eventually patched up between me and my parents, but I always felt closer to Gran that to Mum and Dad. I talked to her almost every day on the phone.

I was just about to head off to start my first term at drama school when my mother told me that my gran had died in her sleep. She had had a heart valve repair sometime earlier and the doctors had suggested replacing the valve, but Gran had refused, saying one heart operation was enough.

The news of Gran's death hit me hard. I was inconsolable. I had been so excited about moving to London to study drama, but now I didn't want to go. What was the point? The only person who had truly loved me had left me.

Gran's death hit my mum hard as well and one night I came downstairs and found her sitting at the kitchen table sobbing. I put my arm around her and for the first time in years we connected. Perhaps something good had come out of my gran's death after all.

Mum and I sat in the kitchen for a while holding each other and then Mum asked me if she could tuck me into bed. She told me how much she had missed doing that and when she took me upstairs and tucked me in I realized how much I had missed her doing it. She sat on the end of my bed and we talked and talked. There was so much to catch up on. Eventually, the subject of drama school came up and Mum urged me to go. I still wasn't sure, but then something incredible happened: the heirloom doll that Gran gave me all those years ago started to play.

When the doll had stopped playing Mum went over to see if she could make it play again. She pulled the cord, but nothing happened. Intrigued, I got up and pulled it, and nothing happened. Then I jumped up and down to see if there was any residual play that could be prompted by some action. Nothing happened.

The next morning when I woke up in my bedroom I thought about drama school and how much Gran had wanted me to go. Then I thought about Gran and how I would never see her again. I started to sob and the doll once again spontaneously burst into song. I was instantly comforted. I rushed to see my mum and told her what had happened. She just smiled and said, 'Not to worry – I think you just had another visit from Gran. Isn't it time you started to think about getting those books on your drama school reading list?'

I'm in my first year of drama school now and loving every second of it. And I feel closer than ever to Gran. The doll has 'spoken' to me on two other occasions and both times I have felt incredibly comforted and supported. It's not just when I'm close to the doll, though, that I feel this comfort and strength. Wherever I am and wherever I go, I have no doubt that my gran is never far from me.

Gifts from the Angels

If you've been reading these incredible stories and wondering why it is that you haven't received signs from lost loved ones, bear in mind that angels can manifest their love in varied and manifold ways. It's entirely possible that an angel has touched your life on countless occasions without you even realizing.

In fact it is extremely rare for angels to intervene directly and ostentatiously in people's lives. Far more common are subtle signs and warnings which, if heeded, can change a person's life forever. Typically these signs are unique to the person experiencing them, as was the case with Peter's picture falling at exactly the right moment in his life, but there are some signs that seem to turn up again and again – signs that are easily recognized and identified as messages from angels.

One of the most common angel signs is leaving a white feather as a calling card. Whenever I come across a single white feather I'm mesmerized. I take a moment to pick it up and caress its softness, and feel truly blessed. I feel a huge inner smile rising, a knowing, a warm all-embracing knowing that nobody who has experienced and acknowledged it can easily deny.

Many people find it hard to believe that a tiny feather can have such a powerful impact, but as Clare's story shows, feathers can not only be a sign that angels are all around, they can also brush your heart:

'Feathers Brush my Heart'

People have said to me that there is nothing harder than losing a child – and they're right. I should know because I lost my son when he was only 14 years old.

I was told that he had died by a doctor in the emergency room. The accident, which involved 12 people, had left three young boys dead and one adult, the driver of the coach taking them to their athletics trials.

I had to identify my son for the officials. I was in a state of shock in the morgue. I was in a sterile, brightly lit room and my son and his best friend were lying on white sheets. As I gazed down at his body, as beautiful in death as it had been in life, I didn't have any desire to touch him because I knew he was no longer there. I just silently and carefully said farewell to the body I had loved and taken such great care of.

Ever since both my children were born I made sure that they only had the very best – the best food, the best education and the best home I could provide. I raised them on organic produce and taught them to love and respect the Earth and their bodies. My son became a gifted athlete. He excelled at school sports and was soon competing nationally. The shelves of his untidy room were crowded with cups and awards. When he was young, as children often like to do, he would bring me little gifts from the garden: a snail, a daisy, a rose and one day a feather. I treasured every one of his gifts and when he brought me the feather I told him that it belonged to an angel. His face lit up and from that day on he was forever bringing me feathers that he found on his way to and from school. He even found one on the path the morning he left for his final trip. I still had it in my pocket as I stood over him in the morgue.

In the days before the funeral I carried that feather with me everywhere I went. Holding it somehow comforted me. When they lowered the coffin into the ground, with tears running down my cheeks I gently let it go and watched it flutter onto the coffin lid. Then a gust of wind blew and the feather returned to me. I kissed it and let it go again and the same thing happened, but this time it flew back onto my coat and rested just above my heart. I knew then that my son was sending me a sign.

I had survived the worst thing that could happen in a mother's life, but I had also experienced the greatest gift – the never-ending love of my son. He is and always will be the feather that brushes my heart.

An angel feather often appears in mysterious places where you least expect it or, like Clare's feather, acts in a distinctive way. Typically it is small and brilliant white, but angels will use whatever is available to them, so the feather may be tiny or as large as a swan's feather. It will be thrown or blown into your path so you can't miss it. However, you need to keep your eyes open to see and feel the angelical realms and need to believe that angels are communicating with you in this way, for if you don't, a hundred angel feathers may cross your path and you won't recognize their significance.

Today, whenever I talk about white feathers being one of the most common angel calling cards, there is always someone who says to me that when they see a feather they can't help but think that it is just a feather and not a divine message. I'm actually quite sympathetic to this point of view, but now whenever I ask for a sign that my angels are around me I receive one, and more often than not that sign is a white feather, clinging to a wall, tree or piece of clothing.

Many people these days will be aware that feathers are angels' main calling cards, but they are not the only ones. Other common calling cards include rainbows, coins, clouds, numbers and messages in the media or unexpected places. Let's begin with rainbows.

How does a rainbow make you feel? In awe? Mesmerized? Rainbows are magical. Every time I see one it makes me stop and stare. Rainbows draw me in and I drink them up with all my senses. These feelings of awe connect me with the angels.

When you are consciously connecting with the angel realms and searching for an angelic sign, you may just find that a rainbow suddenly appears out of nowhere. This is what happened to Julia:

Over the Rainbow

I was returning home from a vacation with my husband. It had been a make or break vacation for our relationship and we had decided that we should split up. There was no shouting or hysterics – just two grown-ups deciding to go their separate ways. I can't put my finger on the reason why we had drifted apart, but the magic had gone out of our relationship. We had married young but now we were in our thirties we weren't the same people anymore. We couldn't find common ground anywhere. Thankfully we didn't have any kids, so our divorce wouldn't hurt anyone but ourselves.

Even though it was the right thing to do it's still a terrible blow when a marriage breaks down. I blamed myself. When the divorce papers finally came through I felt very dejected and alone. I remember looking at myself in the mirror and thinking I looked more like 50 than 30. Although I hadn't been happy with my husband, at least my life had had a kind of routine and structure. Now I was alone there was no structure. Soon I stopped bothering to cook properly and some evenings after work I'd come home and have really strange combinations of food – dry cereal with peanut butter sandwiches, for example. There didn't seem any point in laying the table and cooking.

It was a really low point in my life, but I can pinpoint the moment exactly when the pendulum swung the other way. I was walking home when I looked up and saw a double rainbow in the sky, which was strange because it hadn't rained that day. It was breathtaking and when I looked at it an unfamiliar surge of happiness and energy shot through me. I felt lighter. I called my brother, who lived a few doors away, and asked him if he could see the rainbow, but he couldn't. I knew then that the rainbow was a sign just for me, because my life changed from that moment on. My depression lifted and I started to venture out into the world again. I can honestly say that I am a new person now. I'm not yet in a relationship – although there is someone on my horizon – but whether it works out or not I'll know that I'll be just fine because I know that not just over the rainbow but right here on Earth I am loved.

Of all of nature's symbols, rainbows are perhaps the most awe-inspiring, but clouds can also fill us with wonder with their constantly changing shapes, colour and beauty. As a child, who has not lain down on the grass and watched the clouds, searching for images? I often get inspiration and guidance from the shapes I see in clouds. Sometimes they are better than my satnav and point me in the right direction when I am driving. In some cases the imagery can be so clear, so dramatic, that it can only be interpreted as a sign from the angels. This is exactly what happened to Ellen.

Cloud Watching

My sister died on 7 May 1994. I miss her a great deal, as we lived together for many years before I got married. The hardest thing is that although I loved her dearly I never really got to tell her how much she meant to me. We used to argue so much, but perhaps that was because we were so alike. She was only 23 when she drowned in a boating accident. Even though I've gone on with my life and have my own family now, there isn't a day that goes by that I don't think about my sister and wonder what she would be like now. What would she have done with her life?

One afternoon shortly after Easter weekend I went to visit her grave. As I put my fingertips on the top of the grave, missing her and talking to her softly, I noticed that the sun was fairly low in the sky. I looked up and for a short time a cloud appeared as the outline of an angel with large feathery wings on each side of a tiny body, a floating gown with little feet below it and hands reaching out towards me. It had curly ringlets in its cloud-like hair and its face was smiling. I knew instantly what I was seeing as I had read somewhere about angels appearing in the guise of clouds. Here at last was my guardian angel. It was the most comforting sight to me and for the first time since my sister's death I had the sense that she was trying to tell me she was with the angels and was happy and fulfilled in heaven.

Feathers, rainbows, clouds and animals (*see Chapter Six*) are all natural signs that angels can give us, but they can also show themselves in material things of small value. Finding small coins in unusual places is another commonly reported sign that angels are never far away. Here's Charlie's story:

See a Penny, Pick It Up

If I saw a penny when I was a child my aunt would always tell me to pick it up because it meant good luck all day long. My aunt was like the mother I never had because my mother died a year after I was born. My father had left before I was born, so my aunt was granted custody.

When my aunt died, I missed her love and support beyond belief. She was the only family I had ever known. And when I lost my job a year later due to compulsory redundancies, I missed her even more.

One night I couldn't sleep for worry so I decided to go for a walk. It was a beautiful night and the moon was full. As I walked, I thought about my aunt and wished she was there to give me some of her advice and encouragement. At that moment I looked down and there in front of me in the road was a penny. Without hesitating, I picked it up. I walked on for another half-hour and then I found another penny. Smiling and momentarily forgetting my worries, I picked it up again. It was starting to get a little chilly, so I decided to head home, and on my way back I found yet another penny – a shiny new one this time. I put it in my pocket with the others and walked home.

When I got home I took the pennies out of my pocket and gasped when I read the dates: 1985, the year I was born; 2005, the year my aunt died; 2006, the year it was then! I knew then that the coins were a message from my aunt to let me know that she was still loving, guiding and encouraging me every step of the way. From that moment on I knew that I would be OK.

Charlie's aunt sent a message in a way she knew Charlie would instantly recognize. She had always told him pennies were a sign of good things to come and I'm pleased to report that good things did come Charlie's way. He's now a busy and well-paid freelance journalist and dating a girl who shares his belief in angels.

Unexpected Messages

Angels may sometimes use creative and sometimes humorous ways to grab our attention or make us see things in a different light. For example, my angels often speak to me through the media. Time and time again I've turned on the radio or television and heard the answers that I need to questions going around in my head. I'll turn the radio on, for example, and a song is playing with lyrics that are closely related to a problem I am mulling over in my mind. There are also times when I am inexplicably drawn to buying a newspaper or magazine that I would not ordinarily buy. This is because angels are guiding me towards a message contained within the magazine.

On other occasions I'll be thinking of a problem or a question and then I'll glance up and see a sticker in a window or on the side of a bus or cab, and the words that appear are the answer that I need at that time. One day I went for a walk pondering whether or not I should sell my car or run it into the ground and the first sign I saw in a shop window was 'Everything must go.' And, believe it or not, T-shirt slogans can also be a source of inspiration. Try it the next time you want an answer to a question and you'll be surprised.

Another unexpected place to find angel signs is in numbers. The number 11, especially multiples of it, such as 22, 44 or 55, is a sign that angels are watching over you and trying to open your mind to their presence.

Lost objects found at crucial moments are yet another commonly reported angel sign. I'd like to share Lucinda's story with you here, as I think it is truly astonishing.

Diamonds are Forever

Two years ago I got engaged. It was the happiest day of my life. Sam even got down on one knee to propose. I said yes, of course, and then we both went to see my father, who was overjoyed to hear our news. He then did something really special: he gave us the diamond engagement ring he had bought for Mum 50 years ago. My mum had passed away four years before and Dad wanted us to have it.

Our engagement lasted for nearly 18 months because Sam was in his last year at medical school and we decided to wait until he had officially graduated. I was wonderfully happy until about six months before our wedding, when the diamond in my engagement ring went missing. We searched for it everywhere – in the house, my car, at work, in the garden and the street outside – but it had vanished. I was devastated, but Dad offered to pay for the ring to be reset. It was an expense everyone could have done without, but Dad insisted on sorting it out for us.

After I lost my diamond things were never quite the same. Then about three weeks before the wedding, with the invitations out, the dresses ordered and the venue booked, I wanted to cancel the wedding completely because Dad wouldn't be there. He had died unexpectedly from a heart attack and a wedding just didn't seem appropriate. Up until then he had been a major part of our engagement and our wedding plans, and going ahead without him just didn't seem right.

But then something truly astonishing happened. It was the day of Dad's funeral and, still shaking with grief, I got my black trousers out of my cupboard and put them on, along with a grey shirt and black jacket, and then went downstairs to put on a pair of black shoes. As I did so, I felt something scratching my toe and, thinking it was a stone or something, I took my shoe off and gave it a shake. I could not believe my eyes when the diamond fell out.

I'd worn those shoes many times since I'd lost the diamond and not once had I noticed that there was anything in them. I swear it looked as though someone had deliberately put them there that day so that I would find the diamond on my way to the funeral. When I showed it to Sam he said it was a sign that my dad wanted me to know that even though he couldn't be there physically, he would still be with us at the wedding.

How is it possible that after months of looking for it, that diamond ended up in a pair of shoes Lucinda had worn many times? There are other possible explanations, of course, but Lucinda is convinced that on the day of his funeral her father returned the diamond to her so that she could get married as they had all planned.

Angels love us unconditionally and will always try to find a way to show us they are close by. They can turn up in the most unexpected places and can appear in anything from raindrops to candle flames, wax, soap bubbles and even slices of toast. Just ask your angels to appear and then watch for the signs they send your way.

Some might call all these angel signs coincidences but, as I mentioned in the last chapter, the more you begin to pay attention to these so-called coincidences, especially when they happen in response to a request for angelic assistance, the harder it is to deny the spiritual guidance you are receiving. If you open yourself up to the possibility of angel signs being all around you, you will start to become aware, deep inside, of the luminescent web of love and guidance that can weave its way through your heart and soul.

Another common way for angels to leave a sign of their presence is through inexplicable aromas. Time and time again I've heard stories from people who have smelled a familiar fragrance during times of trouble or when they were in urgent need of comfort after the loss of a loved one. Some of these people previously put these experiences down to their imagination, but when they started to read the stories of other people they realized that what they had always hoped was true – their loved one in spirit had been trying to reassure them and remind them that they were not far away.

Here's Molly's story:

'We are Four'

People always say that children cope far better with death than adults. There's that famous Wordsworth poem, isn't there, called 'We are Seven'? I may get the details wrong, so forgive me, but it's about a little girl who tells a man she meets at a graveyard that she has seven brothers and sisters, even though several of them have clearly died and are buried in the graveyard. The man tries to correct her and asks her how many siblings she has that are alive, but she is adamant that she has seven brothers and sisters. To this little girl there is no distinction between life and death.

My mum died when I was eight and looking back I think my dad, my uncle and my aunt thought I coped very well with it. I didn't cry, I didn't scream, but it was more shock than acceptance. People told me Mummy was an angel in heaven, but for me all that I had left of her was her spectacles, her clothes and her cosmetics.

The day after she died I went into the bathroom and I could smell her everywhere – her deodorant and her shower cream and her shampoo. The shampoo bottle was still open from when she had used it the day before. It smelled like apples. She had used the same shampoo and conditioner on me and I had loved the fresh apple smell and my mum's gentle hands massaging my head and combing through the conditioner. That day, as I put the lid on the shampoo bottle and tidied everything away, I made the decision to stay strong and help my father and my younger brother through this. After all, I was the only woman in the house now.

At night I would cry, but during the day I never did. I knew my father needed me to be strong. There were times when it felt as though the pain was too great, but I never told a soul. Months and years slipped past and eventually things got much easier, although my mother was never far from my thoughts.

It was inevitable, I guess, as my dad is a great-looking guy, that he would eventually marry again, but a part of me hoped that he would at least wait until I left for college or got my first job. But he didn't wait and one day about two months after my seventeenth birthday he introduced me to his girlfriend, Lily. Gently he told me that he had proposed and Lily had accepted.

Just as I'd done before, I put a brave face on things and I gave Lily a friendly hug. Dad asked me if I was OK and I didn't have the heart to tell him the truth, so I told him I was happy for them both. But I was lying. I wasn't happy. I didn't want him to marry. I didn't want the family to be changed in any way. I wanted it to be just the three of us.

I went to my room and hugged Mum's photograph to my chest. I'd been the only woman in Dad's life for the past ten years and now I wouldn't be his number one anymore. I'd looked after him and he'd looked after me. That's how we had both coped with Mum's death. Now, for the first time, I felt truly alone. I felt angry that my parents had both abandoned me. I started to get a headache. Choking back my tears, I went to the bathroom to get some painkillers.

I never took the painkillers because as soon as I entered the bathroom I smelled the most familiar and beautiful fragrance. It enveloped me for a few moments and then it was gone – along with my headache. There is no doubt in my mind that it was my mother. Not only did I recognize her perfume but I also recognized the distinctive smell of her apple shampoo and conditioner, which I hadn't smelled for years, as we didn't buy it anymore. My mother was letting me know that I wasn't alone and that I was still very much loved.

Since then on three occasions in different places I have recognized my mother's fragrance and it has always happened when I've really needed comfort or reassurance. My experiences have helped me accept Lily as a step-mum. They have also convinced me that whatever happens to us in this life the four of us – mum, dad, me and my brother – will always be together as a family in spirit.

Grief and a sense of loss are understandable during the transition period when a physical relationship changes to a purely spiritual one. But, as Molly's story illustrates beautifully, even in death the loving presence of those we cared for in life continues to surround and comfort us. This is a truth that Doreen now understands so clearly:

Helping Hand

I wasn't exactly what you might call a spiritual person. Even when my husband, Luke, died from the devastating effects of prostate cancer I didn't draw any comfort from well-meaning souls who told me he was at peace now in the afterlife. I didn't believe in the afterlife.

At Luke's funeral I felt tired and empty more than anything else. I missed him terribly and now I would have to face the future without him. It wasn't fair, but then I had always known and accepted that life wasn't fair. The funeral was bad enough, but the deafening silence after all the well-wishers had gone proved to be far worse.

I can recall exactly the moment I became an alcoholic and that was the night of his funeral.

Alcohol filled the empty place in my life that Luke had once filled. Prior to his illness, we had been inseparable. We had spent our time working and living together and when we weren't working we were biking in the woods, singing in the choir or walking hand in hand. We loved spending all our time together. Just before he was diagnosed with cancer we had been talking about having children, but after five long years of his suffering I went into early menopause. I was widowed at 44, but I felt 84.

I became very good at hiding my drinking. I don't think anybody ever knew, but I'm sure they had their suspicions when I started to turn up late and dishevelled at work.

One night about five months after Luke died I was driving home from work. My head was sore, my eyes were heavy and all I could think about was having a drink. I turned the radio on and turned it up loud to keep myself awake. I was surprised that the song playing was Abba's 'I Have a Dream,' with the line about believing in angels and seeing something good in everything around you. I'd not heard it played on the radio before and it was the song Luke and I had sung together when we first met.

Missing Luke, I wiped a tear from my face. As I did so, I couldn't believe what I smelled on my hands: Luke himself. It wasn't his aftershave or his medication, it was his own distinctive smell – the smell I had adored before his illness, the smell I had loved whenever I had snuggled onto his chest. To my surprise my sadness was replaced by a feeling of joy. I knew then that Luke was with me, holding my hand every step of the way. How else could I smell him on my hands in my car? The song we had sung when we first met was playing on the radio and Luke's scent was on my hands – the hands he used to hold.

My experience that night changed my life forever – not only did I stop drinking but it was a launching pad to my belief in a world that goes on after we die. Although I know that Luke can never hold my hand physically again, the touch of his hands and the smell of his scent will linger with me forever.

Have you ever smelled a scent that took you back in time or reminded you of someone or something special? Perhaps the smell of popcorn reminds you of your first date or the smell of bread baking reminds you of your grandmother's house? The memory a scent triggers can be instant and, understanding this, angels often try to connect with us via our sense of smell.

Angelic Voices

Angels will also to try to reach us through our other senses of sound, sight and touch. You may, for example, hear someone call out your name and when you turn to look there is no one physically there. This often happens when you are being warned of impending danger or when you need some inspiration, guidance or comfort. You may hear the voice audibly, as if someone were standing right beside you, or you may hear it as a thought inside your head. Sometimes you may even hear a choir of angels singing in your head. This is a most beautiful sound to hear. I'm very familiar with this experience and in my first book, *An Angel Called My Name*, I describe how angelic music and words of reassurance have changed and on one occasion saved my life. The voice of an angel may also have saved the life of Mary. I'll let her tell you herself:

'Go Home'

This happened to me over 20 years ago, but in my mind it feels like yesterday. I was 27 years old and I was heading home from work one evening with two of my colleagues. We stopped at a couple of benches to sit down and catch up on office gossip. Work was so busy there was never enough time to catch up during the day. It was around 9 p.m., but working late wasn't unusual for us – it was the norm.

Nothing seemed out of the ordinary that night. The streets were fairly deserted except for the odd passer-by or group of people heading to a party or social function.

We heard a police siren and it sounded as though it was coming our way, but again this was nothing out of the ordinary in the centre of London so we continued our conversation. I was just about to talk about the Christmas party when I heard a male voice telling me, 'Go home.' It was very clear and very distinct. It wasn't a voice I recognized, but somehow I knew it was a good one. I asked my colleagues if they had heard it and they laughed, saying I needed to cut down on my medication. There was no mistaking what the voice was saying, though: 'Go home.'

I questioned whether I was hearing things, but there was something about the tone or sound of the voice that made me want to obey it. Without hesitating, I grabbed my case and did just what the voice in my head told me – I went home.

I never saw my two colleagues again. Neither of them survived when the driver of the stolen car being chased by the police ploughed into the bench they were sitting on. Every day I live with guilty feelings about not urging my colleagues, who were also my friends, to go home that night. I could have saved their lives. I remember them asking, 'Why are you in such a hurry?' and 'Was it something we said?' but I didn't answer either of them. How could I tell them I was responding to a voice in my head and how could I know that the rest of my life was about to change forever?

I now work to live, rather than living to work. I have no idea why I was saved, but I do know that my angel wanted me to hear his voice that evening.

Like Mary, Jacob also heard the voice of an angel and that voice changed his life forever. This is what happened to him:

'Keep Going'

The year 2001 was a bleak year in human history with the attack on the twin towers. It was also a bleak year in my life. It was the year my marriage failed and my wife left me, taking the children with her. I got to see my kids every other weekend, but it was torture saying goodbye to them when I knew I wouldn't see them again for another 12 days. I missed them terribly. It got even worse when my wife met someone new and the kids started to get really attached to him — so attached that one Sunday evening after drop-off I heard my eldest shout, 'Dad!' and saw him run over to his step-dad. It was the bitterest pill I have ever had to swallow.

I went to bed that night feeling isolated and redundant. I wasn't suicidal or anything, but I was as close to despair as I ever want to be.

Suddenly, interrupting my misery, I heard a tiny unearthly voice so crystal clear and beautiful that there was no mistaking it was the voice of an angel. The voice said, 'You keep going.' Immediately, I relaxed and the next day I felt comforted and in control. I realized that I would never lose my kids because the bonds of love between us were too strong. Instead of feeling jealous, I felt happy that when I wasn't there for my son he had someone else to rely on.

And would you believe it? The next time I went to pick up my kids for the weekend my ex asked me if in addition to alternate weekends I wanted to have them for one evening every week. She said she felt they were happy and settled enough now to cope. I could have jumped for joy.

Whenever I share angel voice stories like these there is always someone who suggests a more logical explanation for the sounds. I've no objection, because everyone is entitled to their opinion – as long as that opinion does not exclude the equally viable possibility that angels can and do speak to us.

Angelic Visions

In much the same way, there are also plenty of rational explanations for unexplained visions. Most of us are accustomed to the tricks our eyes can play on us. In a barren desert the sight of water which isn't actually there is called a mirage. Eyes do indeed play tricks on our minds, but I'm sure you'll agree that the following stories are far more than that: they are angelic visions. In each case the person who saw the angel was not under the influence of alcohol, drugs or other hallucinatory substances and it was easy for them to identity what they were seeing.

Karen was kind enough to write and share her vision with me:

Resting Place

My mother was someone people either loved or hated. I loved her, of course, but I could see how her lifestyle and forthright opinions could alienate others. She was intelligent and generous, but strongly attached to the material things in life. I don't think I ever saw her wear the same outfit twice. It was a good thing my dad had a good job, because her wardrobe alone cost a fortune. She loved reading fashion magazines and socializing. I never asked her if she believed in God. We didn't talk about spiritual things in our household. As I said, it was all very material.

Mum's wicked sense of humour and zest for life was sorely missed when she died from lung cancer at the age of 62. I was distressed during the final years of her illness when she refused to give up smoking, even though it was killing her. She also had no interest in spiritual or alternative healing. Finally, after a period of grieving, I accepted that my mother had the right to choose to live her life in the way she wished.

I cared for her in my home as best I could, but towards the end her struggle got harder and harder. Every day was traumatic, especially as I'm not really the nursing kind of person. On many occasions I told the home help that I couldn't 'do this' anymore, but somehow I did.

One night as I lay in bed I begged for help, not even sure who or what I was making my request to. Within moments I saw the brilliant white wings of angels comforting and supporting me. Suddenly, I didn't feel so alone anymore and I was filled with the strength and courage to complete my time with my mother.

A few hours after she eventually died I went to lie down. I was exhausted but wide awake. Once again I was surrounded by angel wings, but this time they parted and my mother was right before me. She looked beautiful and a good 30 years younger than when she died – the way I remembered when I was a child. There was no trace of the illness about her. She had the most radiant smile on her face and she was reading a book. She was sitting alone in a simple room with a bed and bookshelves made of wood. Through the window I could see lush countryside outside. She looked at me and told me that she wanted me to be happy.

Immediately, the contradiction of this vision struck me. In her lifetime my mother would never have consciously chosen to spend time in a place like that. Yet now this was her place of rest before she moved on to her final destination. I rubbed my eyes and the vision disappeared.

From then on I was able to find peace after my mother's long and difficult final years because I knew she was being looked after by angels in a place of rest and deep healing for her spirit.

I've heard from many people who have been comforted by the vision of angels during times of personal or family crisis, for example when they are caring for a loved one who is dying. I've also heard from people like Chloë, who find that sharing their story can be a source of strength and comfort to others in similar distressing circumstances:

Angels in the Dark

When I was 17 years old I lived with my brother in a tiny flat. I had left my family home when I was 15 because of my father's mental and physical cruelty. I don't know when it started, but I can never remember a time when I wasn't afraid to go to bed. It was in the darkness that he came to abuse me and it was in the darkness that he left me. During the day I daren't look him in the face for fear of being hit. Things came to a head when I was 15 and the social services finally got involved, but it was far too late to rescue the little girl inside me. She had died long ago and in her place was a woman frightened to live. I was terrified of being alone and for two years my brother either sat with me every night until I went to sleep or slept on the floor in the room with me.

When he got a girlfriend I realized that my neediness was causing problems for him, so I told him that it was time for him to stay overnight with his girlfriend. He was uncertain at first, but I insisted.

I regretted my decision the moment he shut the door behind him. It looked so dark inside my bedroom that I decided to sleep on the sofa with the television on. Just before I fell asleep I remember asking God to help me make it through the night.

At about 1 a.m. I was still wide awake with fear. The television was on, but every sound from outside the room made me shiver and terrible memories came back. My mind started to race. What if my father had found out where I was?

I sat upright and as I did so, I felt a gentle touch on my forehead and saw a beautiful face hovering in front of me. I could not see what the face was, as it wasn't clear, but I felt the love it had for me. Then it flew out of the living room and into my bedroom. I followed it and lay down in my bed. I wasn't afraid of being alone in the dark and

I haven't been afraid since. I believe that the face I saw was the face of my guardian angel.

Like Chloë, Asia also believes she saw an angel. Here is her remarkable story:

Angel Children

I was 39 and had just ended an eight-year relationship with the man I thought would be the father of my children. I had put everything into that relationship and when he told me he didn't feel ready to commit or start a family, I felt dead inside. The best years of my life had been wasted on something that was going nowhere. Six months later I heard that he had got his secretary pregnant and they were getting married. I didn't think things could get any worse, but they did when my doctor told me that I was suffering from polycystic ovary syndrome and that it was unlikely I was ovulating. Not only was I single but I had little chance of getting pregnant and becoming the mother I had always longed to be. I felt dead inside.

My best friend – whom I've known ever since we were at junior school together – suggested a two-week holiday in Spain. I declined, but she wouldn't let up, so off I went. Nothing significant happened in the first ten days but it was a relief to be away from everything that reminded me of my ex. Then on the eleventh day I had the most profound experience. I was walking along the beach one evening enjoying the sensation of sand sinking into my bare feet when all of a sudden I felt a love that I had never experienced before. I heard sweet music playing and then in front of me I saw two children playing on the shore. They were running towards the waves and then running away from them as they lapped onto the beach. I could tell immediately that they were not earthly but heavenly children, as they had white hair and wings on their back. As soon as I noticed their wings they turned round and I heard their clear voices saying, 'Mummy, Mummy!' I waved back and they laughed before rising into the air and hovering in front of me. The vision must have only lasted a few moments, but I wanted it to go on. I felt that in some way I was home.

I didn't tell my friend about my vision as I know she would not have believed me, but I did tell her that the holiday was the best thing that had ever happened to me. All my regrets had gone and instead of hating my life or my body I felt gloriously happy to be alive.

One week later I met my future husband. Our attraction was instant and nine months later I gave birth to twins. No one could have been more surprised than me when I found out I was pregnant, except perhaps my doctor, who told me it was a miracle, although he did say that he had heard of cases of women spontaneously ovulating when they had moments of extreme happiness or inspiration.

Ten years later I have two wonderful girls and I will never forget that they are my miracles and a gift from the angels. On that beach in Spain my life changed forever. I was reborn.

As these stories show, people can see angels in many different ways. There is no right or wrong way to see an angel because you will see them in the way that is right for you. Some people may see the wings, face or figure of an angel in their waking or their dreaming life, while others may catch a glimpse of movement out of the corner of their eyes or maybe see even bright sparkles of silver-white light or bright yellow-gold light. And others, like Asia, may see angels every day in the faces of their children.

Another sign that an angel is close by you is a feeling of emotional well-being, a feeling of being loved and cared for. I like to think of this as an angel wrapping their wings around you in a loving hug. You may already have noticed that a common factor in many angel stories so far is an intense feeling of emotional support and comfort. On some occasions, however, this is taken a step further and love and comfort are expressed through the touch of an angel.

The Touch of an Angel

Of all the senses, touch is the most intimate and personal, and anyone who has ever experienced the touch of an angel will know that the experience is as real and as immediate as being touched in real life. Although it is far less common than hearing or seeing angels, perhaps because it is more difficult to accomplish in the physical world, when it does occur it brings profound comfort and incredible joy because it is so unmistakable. The mind can find explanations for sight and sound, but touch is harder to dismiss as imagination or wishful thinking. As Mark explains, it's very hard to conjure up a convincing hug.

Another Place

I was 26 and on top of the world with a great job and a beautiful wife who was pregnant with our first child. Life couldn't have got much better, but then my world disintegrated before my very eyes when my wife was hit by a speeding car. She lost the baby and then two weeks later we shut off her life support. In 14 days I'd gone from being the happiest man in the world to being the unhappiest man in the world.

I'm a scientist and I've never been a spiritual person. My wife was, though, and when we first met we used to have long 'What is the meaning of life?' chats until the early hours of the morning. She stuck to her point of view and I stuck to my atheist beliefs. In fact, we disagreed on just about everything. She was a vegetarian and I was a meat eater. She was into sports and I loved books. I loved action movies but she loved romantic movies and songs – I can't tell you how many times I had to listen to that screechy Dion song 'My Heart Will Go On'. But even though we disagreed on so many things, we just worked brilliantly together. Losing her when we were just beginning our married life together and looking forward to the birth of our first child was devastating. I had no idea how I would recover.

About four months after the tragedy I went to bed and, of course, my wife was strongly on my mind. The nightmare returned and I relived the moment when I got the phone call informing me that my wife was in intensive care and that we had lost our child. My heart felt heavy and sore and I sobbed into my pillow.

Then, while I was sobbing, I became aware of a presence in my room. I couldn't see anyone but I just knew someone or something was close by. Then I felt a pair of strong arms circling around me. They weren't human arms, because they felt silky and soft, but despite being so soft they held me tightly and rocked me gently backwards and forwards. I was instantly warmed and strengthened by this and fell into a deep sleep.

When I woke up I finally accepted the fact that my wife had gone to another place, but that was OK. I knew that I was going to be alright and my wife and child were going to be alright too. Wherever I go and whatever I decide to do now, I will be fine. And don't ask me how, but I know that my beloved family is close by and that we will all be together again one day.

Mark's experience has changed his perspective on life completely. Now he truly believes that love can reach out across space and time and transcend life and death. His story is a moving and dramatic example of an angel's touch, but angels don't always reach out to us in such a direct way. It's more common for them to touch us in subtler ways. If you've ever noticed a gentle breeze on your face when the doors and windows are shut or felt an unexplained tingling on your back, arms or shoulders, drink in the sensation. Your guardian angel could be giving you a loving hug.

Tummy Flutters

Of course, another potent way for your guardian angel to send you a sign is through your stomach. I'm not talking about food here but about gut instinct or that flutter in your tummy which is your gut instinct or your intuition. I strongly believe that your intuition is your direct line to your angels. It's almost like an invisible umbilical cord that attaches you to them and it's perhaps the most reliable way of receiving a one-to-one message from them.

So when you get that icky feeling in your stomach and a sense that something is or isn't right, in the great majority of cases you will be correct. The problem, of course, is that many of us fail to recognize when our intuition is trying to give us a heads-up. It takes a lot of courage, but if we can learn to trust our intuition, as Theo did in the story below, it becomes easier and easier to recognize the guiding hand of angels in our lives.

Not Listening

My brother Mike has always been reckless, impulsive and impatient, whereas I have always been more cautious, studious and practical. Our parents were always thoroughly relieved that one of us had common sense, but deep down I often felt that they loved my brother a little more.

I think the first time I really felt jealous of Mike was when I was six. My mum had given us permission to play with other children at a neighbour's house as long as we were on our best behaviour and said our 'pleases' and 'thank yous'. I did everything that was asked of me, but my brother got into a fight and my mum and dad had to come round and collect us early because he had a cut lip. When we got home, I was completely ignored while everyone fussed around Mike and his cut lip. My dad even joked, with a 'That's my boy' look in his eye, that he didn't like the neighbours much anyway.

In the years that followed, in a desperate bid for attention I'd often come to Mum to tell her that Mike was up to no good in the basement or back garden or that he'd been rude to a teacher at school. But it never worked because however much trouble Mike got into he was always the golden boy. At secondary school he was the guy all the girls fancied and I was just his boring older brother. He started smoking and I warned him of the dangers. He skipped school and I told him he was making a big mistake. I tried to tell Mum and Dad but, just like Mike himself, they didn't want to listen to me. Nobody listened to me.

Over time, Mike grew increasingly tired of my nagging and a rift started to grow between us. Then when he turned 16 he begged Mum and Dad for a motorbike. He told them that he longed to feel the wind in his hair and to whip down the motorway past cars stuck in traffic jams. Much to my relief, my parents refused, but they did say that if he saved up enough money they would consider the idea. So instead of focusing on his A-levels Mike saved all the money he earned from working

Saturdays in a supermarket, mowing lawns and cleaning windows. A year later he had the money and once again petitioned for a motorbike.

My intuition strongly told me that if Mike got a motorbike he would have an accident within a month, but over the years I'd learned to ignore my intuition because everybody else did, so I said nothing. I knew that Mike would laugh in my face if I told him what I really thought. So he bought his motorbike, with my parents' reluctant approval. There were conditions: he was not to ride at night and he was to have proper lessons from a qualified instructor. But my intuition told me that Mike was only ever going to pay lip service to these, and true enough, in no time at all he was speeding around town on his motorbike. I thought about at least trying to talk to him about being careful, but when I remembered his look of wild triumph when he bought the motorbike home for the first time I began to think that maybe he was right and I was just a jealous killjoy.

Two weeks passed after he got his licence and then another, and it soon became clear to me that Mike was actually quite a good rider. I even let him take me on his bike a couple of times and I felt remarkably safe. As the third week passed I hoped that my intuition had been wrong.

But one night a phone call came when I was sitting down to supper with my parents. I answered the phone and it was one of Mike's friends. He sounded breathless but he told me that a truck had ploughed into Mike and he had been dragged several feet along the ground. Mercifully, his injuries weren't going to kill him, but there was a possibility he would never walk again.

When Mike was in recovery Mum and Dad told him the devastating news. I stood silently in the background, but Mike asked me to come closer. With tears in his eyes he smiled weakly through his injuries and said, 'I really should have listened to you this time, bro, shouldn't I?'

I didn't know what to say. I just held his hands and as I did I knew that he would walk again. I told him what I sensed and I could see that it gave him strength.

My intuition proved to be right and with a lot of cursing and groaning Mike did start to walk again. He still limps now but he says that the limp is a reminder to me and to our parents to pay attention to our intuition more.

Many people tell me that they would like to trust their intuition but, like Theo, they often can't tell if it is their intuition or their fear speaking. I believe that one of the best ways to distinguish between your intuition and your fear is that your intuition tends to be simple, gentle and reassuring whereas your fear tends to be complex, loud and self-critical. So if there are long drawn-out explanations in your head or harsh, critical thoughts, it's your fear talking. But if there is a quiet knowing or a feeling

that something does or doesn't feel right, it's your intuition speaking.

Most of us do know what is right – we just don't
think we do. All too often we change our minds and
then become confused. Confusion is a sure sign that you
are not listening to your intuition. Your intuition doesn't
follow a logical thought process – it simply knows what
it knows, no explanation required.

Your body will always recognize and tell the truth,
even though your mind may be saying something else.
So pay attention to how your body responds to situations or to information you receive. Your gut instinct will
tell you when something is right because you will feel it,
like an inner yes.

If you still aren't sure, ask your angels to help you
identify what you are feeling so that the appropriate
action can be taken. This does not have to be a long
prayer or invocation. A simple 'Help me, angels' is
enough. When Eve was in grave danger she asked the
angels for help and through her intuition they gave it to
her:

'Makes Sense to Me'

This happened two years ago when I was on my way
home from college. It was about 7 p.m. on a cold winter's
night and I'd just been to my local shop to buy some

bread and milk. I was walking along the street to my flat when I passed a guy leaning against a wall. I tried to walk past quickly, but he stepped in front of me. He had a broken bottle in his hand, I could smell booze on his breath and he was leering at me. Frantically, I looked up and down the street, but there was no one in sight. I prayed to my guardian angel for help.

Then I looked at my discarded shopping bag on the floor. The bread bag had broken and slices of bread were all over the floor. Suddenly something in my gut urged me to talk about bread. 'Did you know,' I said in a calm voice, 'that the bread in my kitchen goes stale very quickly?'

I can't remember what I said next, but I just kept talking about bread – the price of bread, the kind of bread I liked, how my toaster had just packed up …

My nonsense talk was more effective than a punch in the groin. The drunk took a step back, looking confused, and I seized the opportunity to run away. As I looked back I saw him picking up a couple of slices of bread from the pavement.

I'm convinced my guardian angel helped me that evening. I'm quite a nervous person usually, but the calmness and the words I needed to defuse a dangerous situation just came to me.

Eve's story shows that sometimes our intuition will prompt us to do the most illogical and unpredictable things. But if you stay calm and trust yourself enough to follow your intuitive hunches, you may be surprised to find that everything works out after all.

Look for a Sign

We have covered a lot of ground in this chapter, but the intention was to give you an overview of some of the most common (or should that read 'uncommon'?) signs angels send to remind us of their loving presence.

If you want proof that angels exist, all you need to do is ask for a sign. Then the next time you have a problem, pay close attention to what happens next. Look for a sign. You may see a feather, a stunning shape in the clouds, a significant word, phrase or number over and over again, or you may come across a book that addresses your issue. You may overhear a conversation in a restaurant that seems to hold a message just for you. Or, out of the blue, a friend may call you with the solution to your problem. Soon you'll be hearing and seeing angels in your own unique way.

When I was growing up I often asked the angels for a sign of their loving presence, but it took several years before I could allow myself to surrender my analytic mind and controlling nature and believe what I was experiencing was angelic in origination. So, whenever you ask angels to send you a sign, be sure to also request that they help you to notice and understand it.

Sometimes it helps to test the waters with less important things before you ask for help with bigger problems. So start small. Ask for help finding a parking place at the shopping centre or just the right recipe for an upcoming dinner party. Ask for green traffic lights when you are running late. Then keep a journal or a 'signs from heaven' list of any help you receive from your angels. You'll be amazed at the results.

Feathers, clouds and the brush of angel wings are commonly reported angel signs but, as you've seen in this chapter, angels come into our lives in different ways and they don't just turn up in life-threatening situations, they are with us all the time and can teach us a lot if we learn how to be open to their presence. Angels also come to us on their own terms, appearing to us in ways that are highly personal. There is no right or wrong way to perceive them. You don't have to be a clairvoyant, psychic or medium to experience them either.

If you aren't sure if an angel has left a sign for you, listen to your heart. It will know the answer because when you start to connect with your angels you will start to have the most overwhelming feelings of peace and love. Life gets a lot easier with an angel on your shoulder to guide, inspire and protect you. And all you have to do is ask!

Whatever you focus or put your attention on will increase in your life. So, as you focus on angels, they will begin to make their presence known to you more and more. The more you read about, think about, talk about and dream about angels, the easier it will become to recognize angelic signs and sense angelic presence in your life.

Remember, you don't need a formal prayer or invocation to call angels to your side. Simply think, 'Angels, please surround me,' and they'll be there. Angels are always watching over you. No matter where you are as you read this, you are surrounded by angels. Your room, your office, your garden, your heart and, as the next chapter explores, your dreams are filled with angelic presences. Just look for a sign, and when you find it, believe in it and trust it.

Chapter 5

Night Visions

While we are sleeping, angels have
conversations with our souls.

Author unknown

As angelic calling cards or signs, dreams fall into a class all
of their own. This is because they not only offer an
amazing commentary on a person's life and psychic
development but are also a safe and comforting medium
for angels and the spirits of loved ones to communicate
with us.

If you don't think you dream, think again. Everyone,
regardless of their age and background, dreams several
times a night and it's been estimated that we each have
100,000 dreams over the course of our lives. That's a
whole lot of dreaming. The reason many people don't
think they dream is simply because they can't remember
their dreams. Dreams fade almost instantly from memory
on waking. On many occasions I've woken up with a

wonderful dream still spinning in my head but by the time I've brushed my teeth it's gone. If, however, I immediately record my dream in words in a dream journal as soon as I wake up, I create a permanent reminder that I can use to help myself remember my dream and figure out what it is trying to tell me.

I've been keeping a regular dream journal for the past 25 years and it's grown into an incredible resource. I started with a simple notebook, but the more I thought about my dreams, the more I started to remember them. Soon my dream notebook was replaced by a folder and then by a file and another file. Eventually, when my dream files grew so extensive that they were taking over my personal space, I switched to recording my dreams on my laptop.

Often my dreams don't actually make sense to me at the time but I record them all the same because over the years I've been keeping my dream journal I've found that a single dream is rarely enough. You see, a single dream is often only one tiny piece of a gigantic puzzle and substantially better results are achieved when I analyze a series of my dreams over weeks, months, even years.

It's fascinating to look back and review my dreams and dreaming patterns. More often than not my dreams offer amazing insights into my psychic development, past, present and future. However trivial or illogical they appear, I know that each has a valuable message or insight to offer me. The problem is that this message isn't straightforward but presented in a different language – the language of symbols.

There are many books available to help you figure out how to understand your dream symbols (I should know, I've written one or two of them!) These books are certainly helpful and can help you unravel the mystery, but it is still my belief that the most valuable dream book you can ever use is the one you write yourself – your dream journal. This is because the more you work with your dreams, the more familiar you become with your personal dream images or images that have personal significance to you and you alone. For example, if you are a dog lover, the appearance of a dog in your dream will have very different meaning from someone who is afraid of dogs. Whenever people ask me about the meaning of their dreams – and believe me I'm asked that question a lot – I always urge them to think about what their dream symbols mean to them *before* consulting a dream dictionary.

In fact, interpreting dreams literally can be very harmful. It's a common mistake to make. When my son started school I attended a new parents' meeting and I remember meeting a mother who was looking quite tense. I asked her what was wrong and she said that a week ago she had dreamed that her son had killed her newborn daughter by throwing her out of the window. She was very superstitious and ever since then she hadn't allowed her son anywhere near her baby. I tried to explain to her that her dream was not to be taken literally. It simply meant that her older child was finding it hard to adjust to the new family dynamic and that instead of pushing him away from the new baby she should be drawing him closer.

Another of my friends worried incessantly that a dream about her 18-year-old daughter dying in a car crash was prophetic. She even refused to let her daughter have driving lessons. I did everything I could to reassure her that her dream didn't actually mean her daughter was going to die in an accident. It simply meant that she was ready to make her own way in the world and leave her childhood behind. As the daughter was in the process of applying for college, the dream was a clear message that she was growing up – but this didn't mean she had to grow away.

If you would like to know what your own dreams are telling you, I strongly urge you to keep a dream journal. Significant messages are constantly being given in your dreams and it would be shame to miss them. Nothing fancy is required, just a notepad and something to write with on your bedside table and the dedication to use them.

Dreams really are fantastic tools of self-awareness and spiritual transformation. As I said, the great majority of them I don't take literally. I regard them as a kind of personal therapist, a way to highlight my feelings, hopes and fears so that issues in my waking life can be resolved and hidden strengths and creativity revealed. Sometimes I need to do a bit of self-analysis to get to the real message. I used to feel incredibly anxious whenever I dreamed of people I loved dying or coming to harm in some way. These dreams don't faze me anymore because I understand that in almost all cases the image of death in dreams really does not mean that a person is going to die. It simply suggests that they are going through a period of great change and transformation or that my relationship with them is changing.

Dreams that highlight my feelings, hopes and fears and where I need to do some self-analysis to get to the real message make up the great majority of my nightly dreams, but a small percentage of my dreams have a very different feel about them. These dreams can't be compared to other dreams. They are so lucid and so obvious that taking them literally is the only option. The dream I had about meeting my guardian angel four months after my daughter was born is a good example because it was so amazingly lucid and intense that I'll never forget it. I call such dreams 'night visions'.

If you aren't sure whether you've had a dream or a night vision or visitation from an angel or a lost loved one, remember that the single most important criterion that distinguishes night visions from other dreams is that the experience is brilliantly vivid and impossible to forget. It seems as real as your waking life and even months or years later every aspect, word, message and symbol is remembered in detail. You can't explain how or why, but you know that for one reason or another that dream was more than a dream.

The stories I've gathered together for you in this chapter all fall into the category of night visions or visitations. Each person told me that their nocturnal vision was so clear that the images are now permanently imprinted on their mind and their heart, and the significance of these images has been impossible to ignore.

Let's begin with Katherine's dream.

Words Unsaid

My sister, Mona, passed away with me by her side. She died from septicaemia after an accident at work. I was living in Australia when I heard how ill she was. We'd not seen as much as we'd have liked of each other the last few years but we were still close. It took me a couple of weeks to sort things out at home for my kids before I could head back to the UK and all the time my sister's husband kept reassuring her that I was coming.

Two days before I was due to arrive I got a phone call from my brother-in-law saying that the doctors didn't think she was going to be able to hang on. I did everything in my power to get an earlier flight home but couldn't manage it. When I finally arrived, my sister was in such a bad way I don't think she even knew I was there. She wasn't conscious, so we couldn't even talk. Ever since I had heard about her diagnosis, though, I had been talking to her in my mind, begging her to hang on and wait until I could be there for her. I knew that she would be worried about her children – she had two, aged 11 and 13. I was scared that I wouldn't be able to tell her I would be there for them in any way I could. I was so scared that she would not hear me say those words. Even though she was unconscious when I arrived at her bedside, I kept telling her that her children would be OK and that I loved her and she should not be afraid. I concentrated hard and tried to take away any fear that she had.

She lived for just four hours after I arrived and when she died it was the loneliest and saddest moment of my life. Afterwards I found it incredibly hard to come to terms with the fact that we had not been able to speak and hug one last time. It tortured me that she could have died feeling terrified about what would happen to her children. It ate me up.

As the days passed I can't explain why but it felt as if my life was over too. She had been my younger sister and I should have been there looking out for her, reassuring her. I felt devastated and cheated that so much had been left unsaid. I cancelled my flight back and even though my sister's children had their father and his family to be there for them, I couldn't tear myself away from them. I was in limbo. It was as if my life in Australia didn't exist anymore. I felt that I had to be there for my sister's children instead. My own children, aged five and seven at the time, couldn't understand why Mummy didn't know when she was coming back.

About two weeks after my sister's death I had a dream, but it was more than a dream. It was extremely strange that I was dreaming at all, as my doctor had prescribed sleeping pills for my anxiety and had told me that one of the side-effects was that I would not dream. Anyway, in my dream I walked into a room – it was painted white and completely empty – and found my sister lying on the floor. Instantly, I went to her and rolled her over. Then I put her head in my lap. She lay there for a while with her eyes closed but then she opened them and smiled the most wonderful smile. We didn't say anything to each other. There was no need for words, but I knew that everything was going to be alright. Then my sister pointed to a locket she was wearing. It sprang open. In that locket there was a tiny picture of her children on one side and a tiny picture of my children on the other. She stroked both sides of the locket with her fingertips and smiled again before closing her eyes and falling asleep.

When I woke I could remember the dream in every detail. My sister had been wearing the blue coat that she had worn to her graduation ceremony and her hair had been very long. It hadn't been that long in years. What struck me most, though, was the peace and hope that I felt.

I still grieve over the words that were left unsaid when my sister died, but I know that the dream was a message for me. It was telling me that my sister was fine and she had heard me. I know that now. She heard every word that my heart had spoken to her and she was at peace knowing that I loved her children as if they were my own. She was also gently reminding me that I needed to be there for my children too. I don't know how I heard what she said because there were no words in the dream, but there was communication and I have taken enormous comfort from that ever since.

Every year my sister's children come and spend a large portion of their summer holidays with us in Australia and it is the most magical of times for me. I love to watch them playing together and laughing. I know that my sister is watching them play too and smiling with pride, love and happiness alongside me.

Sometimes deceased loved ones want to visit us and the easiest way for them to connect with us is through our dreams because when we're asleep our subconscious is more open and receptive to receiving messages from the other side. Dreams are also one of the best ways for loved ones to visit us without causing unnecessary alarm, especially to those with a nervous disposition. After my mother's death I longed for her to make contact and the medium she wisely used to do so first was my dreams. It was the best choice for me at the time because I simply wasn't ready for anything else. I had too much fear, tension and self-doubt and this would have closed my eyes and my mind to anything else.

Remember, a dream is something you'll remember when you first wake up. It fades over a few hours and unless you write it down in a dream journal eventually you'll have little or no memory of it. A visitation is an actual visit from the soul or spirit of someone. It seems like a dream, but you will remember it vividly, even if you don't write it down when you wake up. It will stay with you all day and sometimes for weeks and months afterwards … maybe even forever.

During holidays and around anniversaries and birthdays, loved ones seem to make more visitations in dreams. As Caroline's story shows, it's as if they want to share these special days with you.

Lost and Found

My husband, Paul, passed on suddenly on 19 November 2000. When I met him he was not an openly affectionate man. He'd grown up in a very strict, disciplinarian household and his mother had distanced herself from him as a child. She'd rarely kissed or hugged him, believing that he wouldn't miss what he didn't get. It took several years for him to finally let me in, but the struggle was worth it. Our 16-year marriage was a loving and affectionate one. We had three beautiful children and there was far more laughter in our house than tears. But even though he was loving and tactile behind closed doors, in public Paul still found it hard to kiss me or hold hands. This distance did sometimes upset me, but deep down I was aware of how much we loved each other.

Paul's death was entirely unexpected. He was cleaning our upstairs windows and must have fallen off his ladder onto some concrete. I wasn't there at the time, as I was collecting our son from the station, but the doctor told me he didn't suffer and died instantly. He was only 60 and I had been looking forward to getting to know him all over again now our children were leaving home and to growing old with him. But in a split-second my whole world collapsed.

The first few years were the toughest, but the love and support of the children kept me going. It was especially hard on my husband's birthday and on our wedding anniversary. Every year that we'd been married we'd exchanged cards with loving personal messages. Knowing that this kind of thing didn't come naturally to Paul, I treasured every single note he sent me – even Post It notes with kisses on that he used to stick on the fridge. After his death I kept on purchasing cards on special days and in them I wrote the personal things that I had not shared with anyone but needed to tell him. I had to tell him how special he had been to me and how I would always love him. I had to thank him for being a wonderful husband and father and for never letting me doubt his love. I would always close the card by saying that I hoped he was at peace.

Four years after his death on the night before our wedding anniversary I went to bed thinking of him, as always. That night I had an amazingly clear dream in which Paul walked into the bedroom and stood staring at me before slowly smiling. I can't tell you how, but I knew that I was dreaming, so I asked Paul if there was anything he needed to tell me. He smiled and said, 'I want you to know that I am at peace. Don't worry about me. It is beautiful here. I've read all your notes and I want you to know that I will always love you too and that every time you hug our children I can feel the warmth of your arms in mine.'

I woke up with an overwhelming sense of peace and happiness. Everything in my world seemed brighter.

The next day my daughter arrived. She didn't want me to spend my wedding anniversary on my own. When I hugged her I remembered what Paul had said to me in my dream and it was the longest hug in the world. When my daughter finally managed to untangle herself from me she told me that she had had the most wonderful dream about her dad the night before. In her dream she had seen Paul standing in front of her. He was holding hands with a couple of children who must have been aged about seven or eight. My daughter told him that she loved him and he smiled back and said, 'I know.' She looked at him again and asked who the children were. Paul replied, 'I have no idea, but they were lost when I found them and scared of being alone so I've been taking care of them and giving them plenty of hugs. Tell your mother I'm sorry that I wasn't very good at hugging in my earthly life, but I'm getting the hang of it here.' Then the dream ended.

I found my daughter's dream to be as uplifting as my own. Sometimes I wonder who those children were in my daughter's dream, but whoever lost them I hope that they too had a dream to offer them comfort. I also hope that hearing my story will help comfort someone else who has lost a loved one. In fact, I've stopped using the word 'lost' when I speak about my husband because I know now that I haven't lost him at all. He is with me all the time and most especially when I hug my children.

As well as on special days and anniversaries, dream visitations are more likely to occur during times of trauma. I've heard many stories of deceased family and friends coming to offer support and guidance when a person is involved in a major crisis. This is what happened to Holly:

Everlasting Love

My brother, Simon, died 10 years ago. He was 16 and I was 13. He was hit by a car doing 50 mph in an area with a 30 mph speed limit. I didn't go to the trial, but the driver only lost his licence for a few years and had to pay a fine. My parents were eaten up with fury at the injustice, but it went over my head. What was the point? No prison sentence, however long or harsh, would bring my brother back. One morning he was having breakfast with us – stealing my cereal and teasing me as he always did – and the next he was gone forever. The silence in our household was unbearable. Simon had been the talker, the entertainer, and I had been the shy, adored little sister. When he was gone I often thought that my parents wished it was me that had died, not him. He was the talent, the energy and the sparkle. I was just me.

Simon's funeral went by in a blur. Every day, week, month and year that followed it I became more depressed. My parents did all they could to let me know how much they loved me, but the problem was I didn't love myself. I didn't feel worthy of life when Simon's had been taken away from him. My schoolwork suffered. I just didn't care. Everything was gone because Simon was gone. Life seemed too hard. What was the point of qualifications? The struggle to live seemed too difficult.

Things reached crisis point a few weeks before my sixteenth birthday. Being the same age as my brother had been when he died was unbearable. Every night I went to bed crying. I didn't understand why life was so hard and for what? To struggle on? To have life taken away from you by one careless, stupid driver? And what about Simon? Where was he now? Was he in heaven or hell? Was there really life after death? I would have given anything to know that he was alive and that his soul lived on somewhere.

Then I thought, 'No, things like that can't and don't happen. My grandmother died of cancer when I was seven and there was no sign from her. There was nothing, just silence, unbearable silence.' I felt then that I did not want to keep struggling anymore. I just wanted to die too. I thought about going to a chemist's in the morning and buying as many sleeping pills as I could. My parents were going away to a conference at the weekend, so that would be the perfect time. If I could get it right and take enough pills I could end the struggle. I could cease to exist. I could find peace.

I fell asleep exhausted that night and started to dream. In my dream, someone was calling to me out of a white swirl. The voice was familiar and as soon as I recognized that it was Simon's, he appeared in front of me. He looked paler and thinner than I remembered him – but then he had always been a bit on the chubby side.

I reached out to him and he hugged and kissed me. It felt so warm and so real. I was so happy to see him. I couldn't believe it, but it was him, it really was him. I asked him what he was doing there. He replied that it was what I had asked for before I fell asleep. I was shocked and asked him if he had heard me. He said he had. I asked if my love for him helped him and he said it did. I asked him what it was like where he was and he looked at me and said, 'It is breathtaking and someday, but not now, you will find out for yourself.' I understood this to mean that it was not my time to go.

Simon told me that he was fine and asked me if there was anything I needed from him. I told him that all I needed was his love. He smiled again and told me I would always have that. Then he was gone and I found myself sitting up in my bed in awe of what had just happened. I felt a great peace and knew that I would never again consider taking my own life.

I'm in my forties now and there have been many struggles in my life since that night, but I have dealt with them because knowing I'm not alone has given me courage.

I draw tremendous strength from Simon's everlasting love. I know that he is always there, even in the darkness of the night.

Like Holly, after an incredibly powerful dream Nick also found new meaning in the term 'love everlasting'. Here's his story:

Thank You

I was heading out of the door to catch a train home for Christmas. This was the first time in five long years that my whole family would be together again. My brothers and sisters were spread all over the country and we all had busy lives. It was difficult to get us all under the same roof at the same time.

When I was on the train my mobile rang and it was Dad. His voice sounded fragile and he told me that Mum had had a major heart attack. It was touch and go. I was stunned and desperate to get home to see my mother one last time. I wanted to tell her I loved her and that I'd be there for her. Sadly, there were major delays and I was forced to change trains. I arrived home six hours later than planned.

I rushed to the hospital and found all my family standing together around Mum's bed. The doctors had done all they could, but she was slipping away. It broke my heart to think that Mum was leaving us just as we had finally got our acts together and managed to visit as a family again. I held her hand one last time and am sure I felt her fingers move. She died at four minutes past ten in the evening.

That night I couldn't sleep. I paced up and down in my room until the early hours. Eventually at about 4 a.m. I must have fallen asleep because at 6 a.m. I woke up from the most vivid dream I have ever had. Actually, it was more like a vision or a movie playing in my mind. In my dream I saw my mother lying on her deathbed in the hospital. She was surrounded by a lilac-coloured light and she was saying, 'Thank you,' over and over again.

I'd never paid much attention to my dreams before that. I usually didn't remember them or when I did they were so confusing I couldn't make sense of them, but this one stood out from all the rest. I knew it was my mum telling me that she had died exactly as she had wanted, with all her family around her. It had been perfect. That was how she had wanted it.

A few weeks after the funeral I travelled back to my flat and found a letter from Mum waiting for me. She must have written it in anticipation of my visit. It was written in beautiful handwriting and in it she told me how much she loved me and how proud and happy I made her. She had given me a memento of love that I could hold on to forever. I often wonder if in the last few weeks of her life she somehow knew that she was going to die.

Since my mum's passing I have not thought about death in the same way as before. My dream has taught me that love never dies, it just seems to grow and become more enriching. Death can't change that.

Of all the incredible dream stories I've collected over the years perhaps none are as gripping as the goodbye visions where the person who has the dream has no idea that the person in the dream has died. In virtually every case people who have had this kind of dream are convinced that the experience was real. They believe that they were actually visited by the dead and received comfort, warning and, in some instances, a message.

Psychologists often say that such dreams are a product of the grieving mind reaching for any kind of relief from the pain and shock of loss. While there is logic to this argument, it does not explain the dreams where the dreamer has no idea that the person has died. I'll let Jane tell her story:

Staircase to Heaven

When my son Marcus left home it was harder for me to cope than I thought. I tried not to cry as he got on the train to start his new life as a student, but I'm afraid the tears flowed. Marcus, bless him, got embarrassed and couldn't wait to get away. As I watched the train pull out of the station I had no idea what the future would hold for me. My husband still had his job but I didn't even have that. I'd dedicated the last 20 years – the best years of my life – to my children and now, with the youngest flown the nest, I didn't know who I was anymore.

For the first few weeks after Marcus left home I waited anxiously for texts or calls from him. Knowing how much I would miss him, he did call every few days. He had a wobbly start and felt a bit overwhelmed to be living in a city – and to be doing his own laundry – but after a month he seemed to find his feet and really enjoy himself. When he came home for Christmas he was still Marcus but he was a grown-up Marcus. He had his own life now. I was a part of it but not the main part anymore.

Sensing that I was a bit lonely, Marcus suggested that I log onto Friends Reunited and try to pick up with some of my old schoolfriends. I'm a bit computer phobic and was reluctant at first, but when Marcus showed me the ropes I really got into it and discovered a whole new world online. I started e-mailing old friends and made new ones. I hooked up with e-Bay and started trading. Nothing would replace Marcus, but with my new life online I stopped feeling so lonely.

Best of all, I tracked down my best friend, Penny, from primary school. We started e-mailing each other and swapping photographs of our families. Like me she was in limbo, as her daughter had just gone to college. Sadly, we lived some distance apart, so meeting up was problematic, but rarely a day went by without a virtual conversation. I started to think of Penny as my rock and I think she thought of me in the same way.

One evening I was trying to tidy out Marcus's room. There was so much paperwork and junk in there that it must have been close to midnight before I went to bed. For some reason I felt very restless and it was hard to sleep, but I eventually drifted off in the small hours of the morning.

The dream I had that night was one of the most intriguing I have ever had. I was alone in a large building. It felt as though it was a museum and was full of beautiful statues and artefacts. I was surrounded by a golden light. I saw a painting at the end of the room and felt compelled to walk towards it. It was a painting of a large silver winding staircase and there were crowds of people on every step. When I arrived, the scene started to come to life and the people on the stairs started to climb up them. At the top of the stairs there were white clouds and when people reached the top they disappeared into them. Looking down, I saw my friend Penny starting to climb from the bottom of the stairs. She looked so happy and exactly like the photographs she had sent me. I reached out to touch her, but she shook her head. I asked her if I could go with her. Kindly but firmly, she said, 'This is my time and not yours. You need to support Marcus.' I didn't understand, as I'd always supported him. Penny simply smiled and walked on up the stairs without a second glance at me. I watched as she disappeared into the clouds.

When I woke up I felt a bit strange, so instead of getting showered as I normally do I went downstairs to the kitchen to make a cup of tea. I couldn't believe my eyes when I saw Marcus asleep on the sofa in the living room surrounded by bags. I woke him up and asked him what was going on. He told me that he had thought long and hard and wanted to leave college and get a job right away. I was furious. Although I'd missed him terribly I also wanted the best for him and the best for him was to get a degree and improve his job prospects. How could he do this? We'd worked so hard to give our children the best. I told him in no uncertain terms that as soon as I was dressed I was going to drive him back to the station.

I made myself a cup of tea and to calm myself down I switched on my laptop to check my e-mail. I was surprised to see that Penny hadn't been in touch. There was the usual junk mail to search through and then an e-mail from an address I didn't recognize. I opened it up and felt sick to the core when I read its contents. The message was from Penny's daughter and it simply read: 'Mum passed away in her sleep last night. I know how much she loved you all and how much she meant to you, so I'm sending you this message to let you know that her years of suffering are over and she is in peace.'

I had no idea what to think. Was this a practical joke? Penny had never told me she was ill, but perhaps that's why meeting up had been a problem. She had always blamed the distance and I don't travel well so I had accepted it.

I picked up the phone and called her house. All I got was an answerphone message and it confirmed everything. It said that instead of flowers for the funeral Penny had requested money be sent to breast cancer research.

There was so much to take in that I had completely forgotten about Marcus. He came into the kitchen and, seeing me shaken, asked anxiously if I was OK.

'Not really,' I replied, welling up with tears.

'I can't stand seeing you and Dad so upset,' Marcus answered. 'I'll just pack my bags and go back.'

I gave him a hug and told him that I wasn't crying about his decision to leave college but about the death of a dear friend.

Marcus sat beside me and held my hand and as he did so I remembered my dream in every detail. Now I knew Penny had been waving goodbye to me. And then I remembered that she had told me to support Marcus. I looked at him and told him that although we thought college was best for him, he was an adult now and we would support him whether he decided to return to college or not. Marcus reached out to hug me and in that moment we were closer than we had ever been.

The following week, after much soul searching, Marcus did decide to leave college and join the army instead. I felt apprehensive, but I supported him nevertheless. It seemed such a wild decision at the time, but four years later I can see that it was the right one.

I went to Penny's funeral and met her lovely family and they told me that for the past five years Penny had been homebound and one of her greatest joys was chatting to me online. Today, I'm in online contact with three other old friends from my schooldays, but I make sure that our friendship isn't just a virtual one. Whenever we can we meet up and have a good long chat in person about life, the universe and everything.

Doctors and scientists may come up with all sorts of rational explanations for parting visions like the one Jane had of Penny, but through my writing and research I have come to believe that these dreams of reassurance from the recently departed are indeed messages of love and support from beyond the grave. Michelle's vivid dream is another awesome example:

'Time of my Life'

Eleven years ago, after a long battle with osteoporosis, my mother died. My sister and I spent long two years caring for her and when she passed away my sister suggested that as soon as the funeral was over we should both go on a very long holiday to give ourselves time to grieve and also to plan ahead for the future. I wasn't married at the time and there was nothing to hold me back, so we booked ourselves on a flight to Australia and planned to spend two months there.

About a week before we were due to fly out, I lost my nerve. I felt it was wrong to be backpacking around the world as though we were a couple of teenagers and that it was wrong to be enjoying ourselves so soon after Mum had died. I got really negative about the trip and was about to tell my sister I couldn't go through with it when I had a brilliant dream.

In the dream my mum appeared and sat down on the bed beside me. She looked wonderful. Her skin and her hair were glowing and her posture was perfect. Before she died her bones had got so weak she was almost bent double. She brushed my fringe away from my face the way she always used to do when I was a child and said, 'Pull yourself together now. I don't want you to put your life on hold because of me. If you don't go on this trip now, life will flash by and you won't have seen much of the world. Enjoy your life as much as you can. I'll let you in on a secret – I'm having the time of my life over here.' Then she laughed and vanished. Her high-pitched chuckle was so unmistakably Mum's laugh that I could not question the dream.

I told my sister the next day how excited I was about the trip and how I was determined to soak up every moment. And enjoy it I did. I had the time of my life. It was just the tonic I needed after the years of struggle and grief. My sister didn't believe me when I told her, but all these years later I remain convinced that that dream wasn't like any other dream and that my mother really did visit me in the night.

I've heard of enough parting vision dreams similar to the one Michelle sent to be convinced that they are very different from other kinds of dream. Several characteristics mark them out and it can be helpful to know these differences if you have one of your own. First of all, in the majority of cases the loved one who has passed enters a realistic setting, often the dreamer's bedroom, and starts talking. As pointed out earlier, afterwards the dreamer also feels overwhelmingly that their experience was real and that they actually spoke to their loved one. Often the personality of the deceased will be so recognizable that the dreamer is left in no doubt they came to visit them.

Many people who have had such dreams also say that they were greatly comforted by them or were able to make important changes in their lives afterwards. In my experience people who are grieving the loss of a loved one are often in a deep swirl of pain, confusion, anger, fear and guilt. It is unusual for uplifting visions to arise from such emotions, making it all the more likely that the messages of comfort and reassurance that such dreams bring come from a higher source. So if you have had a dream of a lost loved one which has several of the characteristics above, don't assume it's a normal part of the grieving process. It may be that you have indeed received a message from beyond the grave.

Bear in mind, too, that sometimes dream messages of comfort and reassurance don't come to you through the visiting spirits of lost loved ones but through powerful symbols or signs. This is what happened to John:

Lily

We'd only been married 18 months when my wife Jasmine died. She was 30 years old. I remember waving goodbye to her that morning she headed off to work. She was a little angry with me because I'd used the car the night before and I hadn't put the keys back in the place we always put them. We had to search for them for about ten minutes before we eventually found them in my trouser pocket. I wish we had never found them.

She didn't stand a chance really. A madman jumped a red light and the collision was head on. I was told she died within minutes – but that's no comfort; a minute can seem like an eternity.

I had no idea how I was going to face my life without her. We had planned our future together. Now that was all gone. My mum and dad did all they could to help me cope, but I didn't feel I could confide in them. I missed Jasmine body, mind and soul and just did not know what to do with the rest of my life.

One night I had the most astonishing dream. In it – although it didn't feel like a dream it was so real – I was sitting on the end of my bed and a young girl was speaking to me. She was dressed in white and had long white gloves on. She told me her name was Lily and that I should never forget her name.

The day after my dream I met up with my wife's family to discuss the funeral arrangements. We were all in a state of shock but organizing the funeral gave us something to focus on. When we talked about flowers I said I didn't want traditional flowers. I wanted something bright and cheerful to celebrate my wife's sunny personality. But then my mother-in-law said something that made my heart stand still: 'Are you sure? In flower language lilies mean life after death. I think we should have lilies.'

All through the funeral I stared at the lilies resting on my wife's coffin. I thought about the girl in my dream called Lily and even though to this day I have no idea who that girl was, for the first time since my wife died I felt her presence all around me. I've continued to feel it ever since.

I still miss my beautiful wife beyond belief, but instead of crying whenever I think of her I find myself smiling instead because I know she hasn't gone. I know this because I listened to my dream and have never forgotten what lilies mean – life after death.

I've come to appreciate over the years that dreams can easily connect us with loved ones who have passed away. They can do this because they transcend the laws of everyday thinking and bridge the gap between this life and the next. I've also come to appreciate that some dreams can bridge the gap between space and time and present and future. Such dreams are called precognitive dreams.

Ever Had a Dream Come True?

Although most people have never had a dream that has actually come true for them, a small but significant number have had a precognitive or warning dream and some rare individuals have such dreams on a regular basis. Given the fact that you are going to have thousands of dreams in your lifespan, the odds of at least one of them being precognitive are good.

I'm often asked how you can tell the difference between dreams that should be interpreted symbolically and dreams that are truly precognitive. For example, if you have a dream in which your teeth fall out, how can you tell if this should be interpreted symbolically as a fear of ageing, for example, or that your teeth will literally fall out in the near future?! My answer is that dreams that need to be interpreted symbolically tend to be fragments of unconnected images whereas precognitive dreams tend to include entire stories or sequences of events that either have a clear beginning, middle or end or stand out sharply in their clear and accurate representation of waking life. Jo's dream illustrates the latter perfectly:

The Blue Elephant

I was two months shy of my forty-fourth birthday when I found out I was pregnant. John and I had been trying for years but hadn't been blessed. We did consider adoption at one point, but my husband's age – he is nearly 20 years older than me – may have worked against us and it never happened. After much heartache I'd finally managed to resign myself to the fact that becoming a mother wasn't in my life plan. I wouldn't say my life was empty in any way. I had a loving family and husband and a busy and fulfilling working life and then like a bombshell I found myself having a blood test to confirm that I was three months pregnant. You could have knocked me over with a feather.

When you've wanted something for so long and then come to terms with the fact that you probably won't ever get it, it's a huge mental shift to adjust to the fact that you might just get it after all. My whole life had been heading in a different direction and now everything had changed. We were delighted, of course, over the moon in fact, but this didn't stop us worrying about being older parents and whether or not we had enough energy or finances to support a child until it was old enough to stand on its own two feet. Things got even harder when I was warned that at my age my baby was at a higher than normal risk for developmental abnormalities and severe disability. Every parent wants a healthy and happy child and knowing that from the start that your child may be limited or held back in some way by the judgements and prejudices of society is a nightmare.

About a month after I found out I was pregnant my doctor strongly advised me to have an amniocentesis. He told me that the procedure was simple and relatively painless. I wouldn't even need medication or an overnight stay in hospital. My first question was to ask why I had to have this procedure as I knew my sisters had never had them during their pregnancies. My doctor informed me that an amniocentesis could help determine whether a foetus had a chromosomal defect, like Down's or spina bifida. It had been quite a few years since I had read about fertility and pregnancy issues and procedures and I was only vaguely familiar with the terms. But this baby felt like a gift from the heavens to me and I knew I was being forced to make a decision about whether I wanted it to be born healthy or unhealthy. In that instant I had no doubts that I would love my child come what may, but I still agreed to the procedure because if there was something wrong with the baby I needed time to get my head around the idea and make the necessary preparations.

The procedure was relatively simple, as my doctor had said it would be, and by far the worst part of it all was the week-long wait for the results to come through. Before I had got pregnant a week had seemed no time at all, but now, with this burden hanging over me, it seemed like forever. I kept busy during the day with work and 'to dos', but during the evenings and the long nights my mind rehearsed a hundred different scenarios. My imagination was running crazy and all I could think about was how my whole world would change if a genetic abnormality was discovered. I started researching support groups, so convinced was I that my baby had Down's. I've been a good sleeper most of my life but during that week I don't think I got more than a few hours each night. I tossed and turned, longing for the seven days and nights to pass but also wishing they would never end. John was worried about me and how my anxiety might be affecting our baby-to-be.

One night, a couple of days before my test result was due, I eventually managed to fall asleep around midnight. For the first and only time in my pregnancy I actually dreamed of giving birth. My doctor delivered my baby – which was unexpected because I had already been informed of my midwife delivery team – and then handed him to me. I remember looking down at his tiny face and seeing a dimple on his cheek. Then I heard my doctor pronouncing him healthy. My sister came in and she was carrying an enormous cuddly blue elephant with 'It's a boy' written on one of its paws and 'Angel' written on the other. I handed my baby to my husband and lay back in my bed, taking in the details of the delivery room.

When I woke up the next morning my anxiety had gone completely. I felt calm and in control. My husband held my hand and told me that whatever the results were we would get through this. I hugged him and told him that I was fine. I wasn't just saying this to comfort him – I really meant it. I knew that everything was going to be fine.

I really can't explain why or how, but I knew that my dream was a vision of my future. I had never felt so peaceful and calm in my entire life before and although we wanted the sex of our baby to be a surprise when I gave birth, I also knew now that it was going to be a boy.

I surprised everyone, including myself, over the next two days with my resilience and calm and I slept like a baby. As my dream had predicted, the results of my test were negative and five months later I gave birth to a gorgeous baby boy with a dimple on his cheek. Giving birth for the first time is a scary experience, but I felt that I had done it all before in my dream. The delivery room was the same and most eerily of all it was my doctor who delivered the baby, rather than my midwife, who was unexpectedly out of action that day due to a bout of 'flu. The only detail that wasn't accurate was that when my sister walked in she was carrying a tiny bunch of flowers and not a cuddly blue elephant. As for my baby, his face, his tiny hands and his beautiful blue eyes were exactly as they were in my dream.

After staying in hospital for a few days I returned home with my son held tightly in my arms. There was a surprise waiting for me when I got there. While I had been recovering in hospital my sister and my husband had completed the nursery and there sitting in the cot – you guessed it – was the blue elephant of my dreams with 'Angel' on one of its paws.

Jo's dream has left her in a permanent state of awe at the power of her own mind and the invisible forces that direct our lives. Such a precognitive dream experience is rare, though. More common are precognitive dreams that aren't exact representations of the future. Instead, these dreams allow the dreamer to visit *potential* futures. I've come across this kind of dream many times in my research and although they may not be as accurate in their representation of events as precognitive dreams like Jo's remarkable blue elephant dream, they are no less awe-inspiring as they give us the opportunity to either preview important moments in our lives long before we arrive there or experiment with possible courses of action. In my opinion, the purpose of such dreams is to give us greater information so that we feel better equipped to make choices and overcome the challenges that lie ahead. Rory wrote to me about his precognitive dream:

The Music of the Night

When I was about ten years old I went to my first concert and from that day on I longed to be able to learn to play the piano with a teacher who visited my school for private lessons every Tuesday. My mum had died when I was only a baby and my father was struggling to raise me and my two brothers alone. Money was always tight and I loved my father deeply and didn't want to add to his burden, so I never mentioned my musical ambitions to him. I knew we couldn't afford the lessons or the instrument.

One night in my final year of junior school I had a dream. In the dream I was having my first lesson with the piano teacher who visited my school. I wasn't being asked to do anything, but I was loving every minute of it. Then my teacher started to play the first movement of Beethoven's 'Moonlight Sonata'.

When I woke up the haunting melody was still running through my head. The music fired me up so much that I knew I had to talk to my headmistress. She was very supportive and I don't know how it happened, but I was granted six months of free tuition, which would continue in senior school if I showed promise. And true to my dream, in my first lesson my piano teacher simply wanted me to hear and be inspired by an exquisite piece of piano music, Beethoven's 'Moonlight Sonata'.

Far from being stressed that my piano playing would cost too much, my father came home one night with a second-hand electronic keyboard so I could practise every night. Since I listened to my dream I haven't looked back. Music is everything to me and now, ten years later, my dream is to work in the music industry.

Rory believes that his dream wasn't showing him the future, as the future was his to choose, but it was showing him how good things could be if he followed his heart and took music up seriously. I agree with him, as I believe that our dreams can show us potential futures if we follow a certain course of action. If Rory hadn't plucked up the courage to ask for lessons, his dream might never have come true.

Many precognitive dreams only indicate possibilities, showing that the future is not fixed. This even includes those dreams that warn about impending danger. This is because when the dreamer recognizes in waking life the events already seen in their dreams they are often able to change the outcome. This is what happened to Lisa:

Deer Crossing

When I was 23 I was involved in a car crash and my best friend, Grace, was killed. We were both in the back seat when a Range Rover crashed into us. Always the careful one, I had put my seat belt on and had urged Grace to do the same, but she had been tired and had wanted to lie down on the seat to have a short nap, so she hadn't had a chance.

I spent several months in hospital recovering from injuries to my legs, but the injury to my heart was far deeper. I'd known Grace since I was four years old. Life would feel wrong without her to call up and hang out with.

For several years after my crash I would have recurring dreams of horrible car accidents. Sometimes I was in the back seat with Grace and sometimes I was by myself, but every time I would wake up in a sweat. After months of trauma and cognitive behaviour therapy the dreams eventually stopped and when I got married and had my three children I truly believed I had put it all behind me.

Then one night I had another crash dream, but this one was different. In this dream I wasn't in the back seat anymore, I was driving the car. I was driving down a winding woodland road when I ran into a deer. I woke up hearing the dying moans of the animal and feeling blood trickling down my face. The dream disturbed me, but I had plenty of experience of dealing with such distressing images. A month or so passed and the dream didn't return, and six months later I had forgotten all about it.

Then, as I was driving my daughter to a party at a house in the country I'd never been to before, I saw a Deer Crossing sign. Immediately I recalled my dream and I slowed right down. My daughter wasn't happy, as we were late, but everything around me looked so familiar that I felt I had no option. We were coming to a sharp left turn in the road and as I crawled around the corner I saw the strangest sight: a deer was standing right ahead of me in the middle of the road. As I drew closer it didn't rush off as I thought it would, just stared at me. As I gazed into its deep eyes I knew that I was looking at part of my future, but a future that wasn't going to happen because I had recognized the situation from my dream.

Lisa's dream reminds us that we all have the ability to change our future by the actions we take in the present.

Perhaps the most striking precognitive dreams I have uncovered in my writing and research are dreams about unborn children. These stories, which often provide detailed and accurate information about children's personality or appearance before they are born or even before their conception has been planned, seem too incredible to be true, but I have never had any reason to doubt the credibility of such accounts. Peter's story is a thought-provoking example:

'Listen to Me'

In my dream I was sitting on a sofa with a small boy on my knee. He had brown hair and green eyes and a tiny nose. He wanted me to read him a book but I wanted to watch the television. 'Listen to me, Daddy,' he kept saying. 'Listen to me. Paul wants you to read him his book.'

I asked him who Paul was and he started to giggle. I asked him again and he giggled even more loudly. I found myself giggling too. 'Tell me who Paul is,' I said, tickling him.

'I'm Paul,' he laughed. 'Now please can you read me my book? Please, Daddy, please.'

I held out my hand and triumphantly the boy placed the book in it.

I remember waking with a start after that dream. My girlfriend, Sally, was sleeping soundly beside me. I got up and walked around the room. Even though it was dark I could still see all the wedding invitations on the dressing table, ready to send in the morning. Was I ready for this? Marriage? Kids? I panicked, grabbed some clothes and stuffed them into a bag. I went into the kitchen, got a piece of paper and sat there for a while with a pen in my hand. What can you say when you want to leave a woman who loves you and wants to marry you? In the end all I could scribble was one word: 'Sorry.'

I booked a flight to Germany that night to stay with my brother. I needed time to think and clear my head. Everything had been moving too fast for me in the last few months. When I arrived at my brother's flat he urged me to call my girlfriend at least to let her know I was alright, but I didn't have the stomach for it. Eventually he did it for me. He told me that she was in pieces. This just made me panic even more.

Now, five years later, when I think about that week in my life I'm ashamed of myself, but back then I thought I was doing the right thing. I didn't think I'd make a good husband or a good father. I loved my girlfriend and wanted to marry her one day, but she seemed to be in such a hurry. I ended up staying in Germany for six months and when I eventually went back to the UK to start a new job I heard that my girlfriend had moved up north and was seeing someone else.

A year or so later everybody I knew seemed to have lost touch with her. I had had a few casual relationships, but there was always something missing. I started to think more and more about Sally, and the more I thought about her, the more I longed to see her. But would she want to see me?

I eventually managed to track her down through her sister. When I first got in touch her sister hung up the phone, but eventually she agreed to meet me. When we met up in a coffee bar I told her that I didn't expect Sally to forgive me, I just wanted to know she was OK. I asked if she was married yet and her sister nodded. A part of me was happy for Sally, as she had always longed to marry, but another part felt empty. There was no place for me in her life anymore. I thanked her sister for talking to me and promised to leave Sally alone. Then the strangest thing happened. Her sister bit her lip hard and then told me to come round the following Saturday. I asked why and she said that there was a whole stack of things in storage that I needed to collect from when I had been living with Sally.

Saturday arrived and I rang the doorbell. A little boy answered and I instantly recognized him as the boy in my dream all those years ago. It was uncanny. He had the same brown hair, green eyes and cutest button nose. He was very confident and shouted, 'Mummy, man at door,' then bounced away.

'I'm coming, Paul,' a familiar voice replied, and before I knew it I was standing face to face with Sally.

The next few moments felt like an eternity, but somehow we ended up embracing. It turned out that Sally wasn't married at all. Her sister had just told me that to put me off, but because she wanted to give Sally a chance to make up her own mind about me she had also arranged for me to call round at a time when she knew Sally would be in.

Then Sally did the most incredible thing: she forgave me. I didn't deserve it, I know, but now I am dedicated to spending the rest of my life making her and my son – and yes, it turned out that the little boy in my dream was my biological son – the happiest people in the world.

Peter's story sounds like the script for a movie, but whenever I read it I'm reminded of the strange and beautiful ways in which the dreaming mind works and the stunning proof it offers that we are all spiritual beings with the ability to communicate across the physical boundaries of space and time.

Night-time Adventures

I can clearly recall when my fascination with dreams and dreaming began. I must have been about nine and had just watched the first of many viewings of *The Wizard of*

Oz. I went to bed that night longing to create the magical Land of Oz in my dreams.

Sadly, I haven't managed to visit Oz yet, but I've visited some pretty incredible places in my dreams. I've met my guardian angel and my late mother in them and these experiences have convinced me that angels and spirits can communicate with us through our dreams. My night-time adventures have also taught me that paying attention to my dreams is one of the safest and gentlest ways for me to develop my creativity and boost my self-confidence, especially through lucid dreaming.

Lucid Dreaming

Lucid dreaming simply means being aware that you are dreaming. If you've ever had this experience, you'll know what a thrill it is. If you haven't, let me tell you that it is incredibly liberating. In a lucid dream you are in control of what happens and you can go anywhere, do anything or be anything that you want. You can also visualize possible solutions to dilemmas in your waking life and try out different approaches and situations.

Some people are lucky enough to be able to lucid dream with relative ease, but most of us, me included, have to work at it by using certain techniques, like getting into the habit of asking yourself 'Am I dreaming?' every time something unusual happens to you in your waking life and your dreams. An essential step, of course, is to believe you can take charge of your dreams.

I had my first lucid dream in my late twenties. I'd just completed a psychic development course and was keen to practise my new techniques. Every night before I went to bed I reminded myself to ask the question, 'Am I dreaming?' in my dreams. After three or four weeks I started to give up hope as although my dreams were as colourful as ever, I still couldn't take charge of them. I wasn't aware that I was dreaming when I was dreaming. Then one Saturday night things finally fell into place. I went to bed at about midnight, only to be awoken at 4 a.m. by the loud wailing of two cats outside my window. I knocked on the window and they ran away, but when I went back to bed I was wide awake. I tried to doze off, but it was impossible, so I got up, made myself a cup of tea and spent an hour or so reading and tidying up my paperwork. At around 6 a.m. my eyes started to feel heavy and I went back to bed, feeling relaxed and incredibly grateful that it was Sunday and I could lie in as long as I liked.

I didn't know it at the time, but some experts believe that rearranging your sleep pattern in this way is one of the best methods of encouraging lucid dreaming. This is because during periods of delayed sleep we tend to have more REM or rapid eye movement time (the stage of sleep when you are most likely to dream) than we would have had if we were sleeping at our normal time, and as a result there is an increased likelihood of lucid dreaming.

I slept for a further two hours that Sunday morning and during that time I became aware that I was dreaming. I was flying over London and for a while I experimented with spinning, turning, ducking and diving, but somewhere along the way I lost my confidence, nose-dived into the London Eye and woke with a start. Although my lucid dream had been cut short, it didn't seem to matter. I had made a vital breakthrough.

A few weeks later I realized I was dreaming about flying again and with my confidence renewed I literally soared. This time I flew over Paris before heading to New York. With so much to explore and so many sights to see there was no way I was going to let my ability to lucid dream go.

Now I lucid dream a couple of times a month. Every time I feel refreshed and energized by the experience and I've received hundreds of accounts from other lucid dreamers who feel the same.

Lucid dreaming is certainly a wonderful confidence-builder, but there is another type of night-time adventure which has absolutely convinced me that there is more to us than our physical bodies, and that is an out-of-body experience, or OBE.

Out-of-Body Experiences

I've only had one out-of-body experience to date, but it has provided me with a rich and deep resource of spiritual awareness. I had just turned 40 at the time and had had a really busy day travelling long distances for radio interviews. I fell asleep on my stomach at about 1 a.m., but I soon became aware that I could see the ceiling above me, even though my head was buried in the pillow. My body started to gently vibrate, but perhaps because I was so tired I didn't feel anxious at all. I stayed calm and then I was free. I had somehow climbed out of my body.

Hovering above myself, I noticed that I had put my nightdress on inside out and I smiled, remembering how clumsy and tired I had been as I had stumbled into bed. There was my husband lying next to me, snoring away as usual. I then had a good look around my bedroom and made a mental note to tidy up in the morning. The place was a tip. I thought I'd wander around the house a bit, just to test myself, and off I went down the stairs and into the living room and then the kitchen. Then I thought about taking a look around the garden and as soon as I thought it I was there. I noticed a cigar butt on the garden bench and decided to confront my husband about that in the morning. He had promised to give up smoking. Then I thought about the flowers in the garden and at once I was floating high above the garden looking down at it from a different angle. I knew I could go a lot further and a lot higher than this, but then I thought about my children. At once I was in their bedroom and floating just above them both in their beds. My son was moving gently and my daughter was pursing her lips in her sleep. I decided I had had enough for one night and at once I found myself back in my sleeping body.

Many different names have been given to the entity or spirit that 'travels' outside the body and these include 'astral body', 'dream body' and, my favourite, 'soul body'. Out-of-body experiences have themselves been variously called 'astral projection', 'dream travel' and 'boarding the spiritual plane'. Some people argue that the experience is actually a dream, but to anyone who has ever had it – and I know from my research that there are thousands of you – it is so much more than a dream. It is a spiritual awakening.

Sleep Working

While we are discussing the subject of spiritual awakening I'd like to conclude this chapter by mentioning another remarkable category of dreams. These are dreams about working in a spiritual job while you are asleep.

People who have these dreams say that several times a month they find their non-physical bodies undertaking spiritual assignments such as helping dying people pass to the other side, helping people to heal or cope with challenges or offering encouragement and strength to those who are feeling weak and vulnerable. It isn't just people in the helping or healing professions that have these kinds of dreams – anyone can have them. I have received accounts of such dreams from people in all kinds of professions, from doctors, nurses, teachers, paramedics and social workers to lawyers, estate agents, executives, tax officials and, yes, even traffic wardens. Some of them say that several times a month they find themselves tending to those in need and although in most cases the task they are assigned in their sleep stays the same, it can sometimes vary.

Stephanie sent me this story a few years ago and I'm including it here because it is a brilliant example of these 'spiritual assignment dreams':

'Hold my Hand'

It happens once or twice a year, sometimes more. I know when it has happened because when I wake in the morning I feel quite drained. Fortunately, my energy returns in a few minutes and during those few moments when I regaining my strength I recall exactly what happened in the night. During the day I'm a sales rep, but during the night my spiritual body helps others pass over to the other side; my dream job is to ease their transition.

Just last week I helped a couple pass over after a terrible car crash. They were both confused and disorientated and still sitting in the car when I arrived. The man refused to believe he was actually dead, but I was with them every moment comforting them and reassuring them everything would be OK. I gently guided them out of their bodies towards the light and the following morning I heard about their accident and their deaths in the news.

The strangest thing is that it isn't the people I'm closest to in waking life that I help in my sleep. My grandfather passed recently and I wasn't called to assist him, even though we were very close. This doesn't upset me because when I go about my spiritual dream work I feel close to everyone, not just my nearest and dearest. It feels as if the people I am helping are my family, even if they aren't in waking life.

My night-time experiences have truly taken the sting out of death for me and I know that when my time comes there will be a brother or sister or loved one in spirit there to hold my hand and guide me just as I've been guiding others.

When I first heard about these dreams about 30 years ago it didn't occur to me that they might be anything other than dreams, but over the years I have heard so many people tell me about the spiritual work they do in the night that I am now convinced that they are real experiences. I haven't any recollection of them myself, but if our consciousness can explore, learn and grow in our sleep there is the strong possibility that many of us are drawn to spiritual or healing work then.

Have you ever woken up after a good eight- or nine-hour sleep feeling a little worse for wear? There may be emotional or medical reasons for this (which should, of course, be checked out by a doctor), but if you can't think of any rational explanation for your fatigue you may want to consider the possibility that your spiritual body has had a very busy night indeed. Perhaps you were the angelic presence that helped a newly deceased person pass over? Or perhaps your non-physical body offered others encouragement, comfort or healing in some way? It's a truly beautiful thought that when we sleep we all have the potential to become angels and hold the hands of those in need.

Sleep Well and Dream Out Loud

Many of us lead busy lives and pay very little attention to our sleep, but it can be as exciting as waking reality, as we have far greater access to memories, impressions, truths and spiritual awareness when we dream than when we are awake. Also, when we sleep the barriers of logic, disbelief and negative thinking are lifted and our psychic perception and vast potential are given the chance to be expressed. That's why I highly recommend that you pay more attention to your night-time adventures.

Remember that if images should appear that frighten you or upset you, you should stay calm and try to understand what the purpose of those images is, because in the great majority of cases your dream images are not meant to be interpreted literally but symbolically. And if you do have a night visitation or a psychic dream, remember that it will feel very vivid and totally different from a normal dream. It will also feel energizing and comforting. And if you still aren't sure if an angel has visited you in your dreams, trust your heart – that is the best truth detector of all.

Chapter 6

Loving Animal Angels

> I swear I think now that every living thing without
> exception has an eternal soul. I swear I think that
> there is nothing but immortality.
>
> **Walt Whitman**

You may have noticed that all the stories so far in this
book have a common theme and that is clarity emerging
from confusion, order coming out of chaos, pain turning
to hope and certainty arising from doubt. Many of us
today feel confused and uncertain and it is all too easy to
believe that everything that happens to us is chaotic.

Atheists present chaos theory as the ultimate answer
to anyone who believes their life is something more than
a random event, but in the last few decades scientists
have discovered a new meaning to chaos theory which
suggests that there *are* subtle patterns to chaos. Take the
miracle of DNA, for instance, or the human circulatory
system, or the intricate design of a snowflake. There is

nothing random there, just a perfect design in which everything has a place, function and purpose. To illustrate the point further you only need to look at the natural world, where patterns and an unexplained intelligence can often be seen. Take salmon, for example – just how do they find their way to their spawning grounds every year?

Many natural miracles happen without human intervention, but there are also many that show there is a powerful connection between humans and nature. Dolphins, for example, have long been known for their ability to connect with and heal humans. It's always been a dream of mine to swim with dolphins and two years ago that dream became a reality when I swam in Florida with a dolphin called Leister. Holding on to his slippery fin and skimming through the water was an unforgettable and deeply spiritual experience. I've read many amazing stories which suggest that dolphins can sense the feelings or problems of humans and now I can understand why. But it's not just dolphins that can connect with humans and sense our need for healing. I've heard incredible stories about countless different kinds of animals and each story offers inspiring lessons of patience, trust, compassion, healing and love.

I believe that animals are divine messengers with spiritual truths to teach us both in this life and the next. I sincerely hope that my brief selection of extraordinary true animal stories will help you find comfort in the face of challenge or loss and recognize the interconnectedness of all living things.

Jackie wrote and told me the amazing story of her collie Sandy:

Sandy

When I was growing up I begged and begged my parents for a dog. I was an only child and a dog would have meant the world to me, but my parents both worked full time and it wasn't practical. I accepted that it wasn't possible, but when I got married and finally had a place of my own, one of the first things I did with my husband, Austin, was buy a dog. We were thinking about starting a family fairly soon as well, so I did my research and decided on a collie, as they had the reputation for being good with young children.

I found out I was pregnant the same week that I made an appointment to see a responsible collie breeder. When I explained my situation, the breeder wisely steered me away from a puppy and suggested an 18-month-old collie called Sandy instead. I had had my heart set on a puppy, but I agreed to take a look at Sandy. I was ushered into a room and there was a nose pushed up against a wire grate and a mass of black and white fur behind it. The wire grate was lifted and Sandy took a few tentative steps towards me. I stared into her deep brown eyes for a few moments and she stared back into my brown eyes. It was love at first sight. I picked her up, buried my face in her neck and told her she was coming home.

Sandy soon became a part of the family and Austin and I loved taking her for walks and playing with her in the back garden. We tried to get her to sleep in the kitchen, but she preferred sleeping in the spare room – the room that was being prepared as a nursery. At first there were so many ladders and shelves and paint pots around that there didn't seem to be enough room for her to sleep there, but as long as she had a cushion she didn't seem to mind.

My pregnancy was textbook perfect until the last ten weeks or so when I started to feel really tired and then about eight weeks before my due date I went into labour and was rushed into hospital. My son Aaron stopped breathing within minutes of birth. Terrified, I watched his tiny lips turn blue, but he was resuscitated and placed on a ventilator. He spent the next few weeks in the neonatal intensive care unit and when he finally came home he was placed on an apnoea monitor. An oxygen canister, a suction machine and all sorts of medical equipment were set up in the nursery and a nurse visited daily to help us care for him.

When the nurse made her first visit she noticed Sandy's cushion in the nursery and told us to remove it immediately. We told her that Sandy was gentle and loving, but she gave us strict instructions to keep her away from Aaron. So, for the first time since she had been brought home, Sandy had to sleep in the hall with the door to the nursery shut. It was heartbreaking, but we wanted to do everything we could to make sure no harm came to Aaron.

Two weeks later at about 4 a.m. Sandy woke me up by pawing at my bedroom door. She had done this a few times before and it had been because she needed to go outside to relieve herself. Heavy with sleep, I resigned myself to taking her out on her collar, so I put my coat on. When I opened the bedroom door and headed downstairs to unlock the back door, though, Sandy didn't follow. She just sat at the top of the stairs barking. By now Austin was awake, wondering what on Earth was going on. I came back up the stairs and Sandy ran to the nursery door and started pawing at it and barking. I was tired and annoyed by now and tried to pull her away from the door, but having only recently given birth I just didn't have the strength and asked Austin to help.

What Austin did next surprised me. Instead of dragging Sandy away, he opened the nursery door. We both watched as Sandy jumped up with her paws on the side of Aaron's cot. I went towards the cot to grab her collar and pull her away, and as I did so I glanced down at

Aaron to check that he wasn't awake. Instantly, I knew something was wrong. Aaron wasn't breathing.

I pulled Aaron's limp body out of the cot and my husband called the hospital. I tried to blow some warm breath into my baby's blue lips. There were tears running down my cheeks and with all my heart I pleaded for Aaron to breathe. Then I heard the most beautiful sound I have ever heard – the sound of Aaron coughing. I turned him over to help clear his lungs and he started to cry. By now the paramedics had arrived and they checked him over and told me he was fine. They did tell me that I got to him just in time, though – a few minutes more and he might have died. The relief was overwhelming, but it was soon overtaken by anger. Why hadn't the monitor gone off?

It turned out that there was a fault in the equipment and it is terrifying to think that that tiny fault could have killed my son. Shaking and exhausted, I went to my bedroom and held Aaron close to me. Sandy was waiting for me and it was then that I realized that she had saved my son's life.

The following evening I tucked Aaron into his cot and then stooped down to give Sandy a big hug. I moved her favourite cushion back into the nursery and two years later that is where she still sleeps every night.

Dogs do seem to sense when people are in danger and their deep devotion to their owners can often save lives. Sadly, the papers seem to be reporting an increasing number of terrifying stories about dogs turning against their owners and even taking the lives of babies and children. These stories make chilling reading, but more often than not it is the treatment of the dog by the owner that is to blame. In our treatment of our pets and all animals I believe that nothing less than the direction of life itself is at stake. If we continue to treat animals with selfishness and cruelty, we will continue to create a world of suffering and we ourselves will suffer the devastating consequences of that decision. What is precious about life can only grow from honouring and respecting all forms of life.

This next story, sent to me via e-mail by a lady called Tamsin, features another much-loved household pet, the cat.

Whiskers

I guess I must get first prize for the most unoriginal name for a cat, but if you saw Whiskers you would understand why she has such an obvious name. She has the tiniest little bony head but the most enormous pair of whiskers I have ever seen on a cat. Sometimes they seem to drag her down because they are so long and everyone who sees her comments on them.

Whiskers has always been a much-loved member of our family, but we had no idea how important she was until my three-year-old daughter Lara fell ill with a severe chest infection. The doctors tried everything from antibiotics to inhalants, but nothing seemed to work. Finally they suggested moving her to hospital. I was apprehensive about letting her go but realized it was the right thing to do, so arrangements were made for her to leave first thing in the morning. I sat up all that night with her, holding her hand. She had lost several pounds since her infection and was so frail I began to fear the worst. As I sat there with tears running down my cheeks, I felt lost and afraid.

I must have fallen into a deep sleep holding Lara's hand because when I woke up it was morning. I looked at Lara and could see that Whiskers was lying on top of her. At first I panicked, but then I saw how carefully Whiskers had arranged herself on Lara's chest, almost as if to comfort her. I bent over them both and Whiskers woke with a start. Then Lara started to wriggle and mutter to herself. I could not believe it when she reached out her hand towards me and smiled. I shouted for my husband, who came running into the room, and explained to him how Lara had come back to life after Whiskers had lain down on her.

For months afterwards I could not decide whether it was a coincidence or something greater than that. I got my answer when I had a severe migraine attack. I used to have migraines when I was a child and they would last for days. But Whiskers helped me with this one by curling up beside me and within half an hour my head pains had gone completely.

Shirley's story is similar to Tamsin's in that her cat was also able to sense and heal her pain:

Spook

I've always been a cat lover and since I got my first cat when I was three years old, I can't remember a time when there wasn't one in my life.

I got Spook when I was 19 years old. I called her Spook because she was completely white, like a ghost, apart from a little splash of black fur on the right side of her nose. She came with me when I left home and she was with me through college, through several broken hearts, through redundancy, marriage and pregnancy. She was with me when I brought my daughter Victoria home.

I'd had a very difficult birth and in the weeks that followed, as my husband and I struggled to adjust to parenthood, our relationship broke down. We tried to work it out, but when he had an affair I could tell that it was over between us. So there I was, an inexperienced mum with a six-month-old baby to care for alone. I would cry for days, weeks, on end.

Victoria was a fussy baby and would only sleep for a few hours at a time. When she was awake the only thing that would stop her screaming was being walked around and gently bounced. If I tried to do anything else when holding her, like listening to the radio or reading a magazine, she would scream. It was an ordeal. She demanded every bit of my attention and I have to admit that I started to resent her. I wasn't sure whether I loved her. I even considered adoption, I was feeling that low.

At first when I brought Victoria home Spook was wary. She found the sound of the baby crying unsettling and would scuttle out of the room. 'That makes two of us,' I remember thinking. Despite feeling nervous, though, she would never be far away. Whenever Victoria was asleep, instead of sleeping on her cosy blanket, as she always used to, she would curl up beside me, purring loudly.

One day as I tiptoed out of the nursery, having spent the last hour or so trying to get Victoria to sleep, I stepped on a musical toy and its merry chimes set Victoria off crying. This was the last straw and instead of rushing to her side I just sat down, put my hands over my face and cried and cried.

After a few moments I felt whiskers and a wet nose touching my hands. It was Spook. You have no idea how unbelievably comforting she was to me at that moment.

She jumped onto my lap as if to encourage me to settle Victoria. Feeling stronger and calmer, I got up, lifted Victoria out of her cot and started to rock her. She was back asleep within minutes

I didn't realize at the time how difficult it had been for Spook to come up to me like that. Screaming and crying had always unsettled her deeply and there she had been in the nursery with the baby and me crying together. But after that precious moment she lost her fear of Victoria and was constantly by my side, whether Victoria was screaming or sleeping. When Victoria did start crying I knew that that was the last place Spook wanted to be, but her constant companionship, love and courage inspired me to go the extra mile and show my love for Victoria.

Victoria is 16 months old now and Spook will even let her stroke and hug her. I know she hates it when Victoria pulls her tail, but she takes it all in good humour. Once again she is teaching me invaluable lessons about love and understanding.

Shirley was extremely grateful for the love and attention of her cat during a particularly difficult time in her life. She believes there is a strong connection between her and her cat, and her story is yet more proof that angels can and do work with pets and wild animals in much the same way that they work with human souls in this life, souls in the afterlife and natural elements like plants, flowers, trees, oceans and the breeze.

If you want to feel closer to angels, spend some more time with your pets or in nature or green places – this is perhaps one of the easiest ways to raise your spiritual energy. Have you ever felt an angel's breath in the gentle breeze? A teardrop in the falling rain? Heard a whisper amongst the rustle of leaves? Or been kissed by a lone snowflake? Nature is an angel's favourite hiding place. And our pets, whether they are cats, dogs, rabbits, horses, hamsters or goldfish, are also part of this angelic tapestry.

Angels speak to us in many ways and send their messengers in many forms, but whatever form they choose it will always be something significant to the person the message is for. Animals can clearly be divine messengers, but angels can also work their magic through wild creatures like birds. We're all familiar with stories about cats, dogs and horses sensing danger or saving lives, but was Malcolm's son saved by a rescue Robin?

Rescue Robin

I had a crucial deadline to meet at work and the timing couldn't have been worse for me to take a day off to look after Gary, my two-year-old son. My wife normally looked after him, but she was laid low with a nasty 'flu. I couldn't call Mum and Dad because they were on holiday and my wife didn't want to hire a babysitter. So there I was singing nursery rhymes and playing puzzles when my colleagues at work were tearing their hair out.

I spent the morning trying to wear Gary out in the hope that he would fall asleep so I could at least get a few hours free to catch up on my e-mails. My master plan worked and after sausages and ice cream for lunch Gary suddenly fell asleep on the living-room sofa while watching TV. I switched the TV off, covered him with a blanket and seized the moment to escape to my office.

I was busy working through my e-mails when a sound startled me. I spun round. There was a red-breasted robin sitting on the window sill and chirping and warbling with great vigour. This had never happened before. I was used to birds flying away whenever a human was in sight, but this one could clearly see me and didn't seem bothered. His little red chest was heaving and I got up to check that he wasn't in distress. I got really close to him and still he didn't fly away, just chirped harder. Then, when I reached out to lift the window latch, he jumped down from the window sill and started hopping and fluttering around on the grass.

Even though I had stacks of work to do, I didn't want my first robin sighting of spring to end so quickly, so I went to the back door to see what was going on with the bird, and that's when I heard another startling sound. Something was splashing in the paddling pool. It was

Gary. He wasn't in any danger, but there is no telling what might have happened if he had stayed in the water for longer. I pulled him out and hugged him tightly, cursing my thoughtlessness in not locking the back door.

Was this rescue robin an angel? I don't know, but now I keep my eyes and ears open for the signs nature sends me.

Another remarkable bird story was sent to me by Anne, whose father was a devoted bird lover:

Sparrow Fingers

My dad always looked fierce, but underneath he was a big softie. He loved animals, especially birds, and taught me to respect them. On many occasions when I was growing up I can remember him bringing home yet another injured bird to nurse back to health. My favourite picture of him is one in which he has a sparrow sitting on his fingers and our cat sleeping in his lap.

Dad died from an unexpected heart attack at the age of 76. I knew, of course, that one day my parents would die, but Dad had been in such good health I thought he would go on forever. I missed him deeply. My mum was really cut up about it too and I was worried about her. I asked her if she would like to move in with me and my husband so that she wouldn't be alone, but she refused.

A month after my dad died things took yet another turn for the worse when my husband was taken very ill with a bout of pneumonia. It was touch and go and I was absolutely terrified that I was about to lose another important man in my life. I didn't think I could cope with that. He was transferred to hospital so he could get round-the-clock care and I had no choice but to sit and wait for news.

One day, to clear my spinning head, I decided to take a walk around the hospital gardens and I noticed a sparrow following me. For some reason I can't explain I felt drawn to the bird. It came closer and closer to me and clearly wasn't afraid. The next day when I went to the gardens it was there again and the same thing happened. It happened again on the third day, and then on the fourth I heard the news I had been longing for: my husband was in the clear. I could take him home the following day.

My husband made a slow but steady recovery once he got home and this was when things started to get really strange. I was clearing away some rubbish in the backyard one day when I saw the sparrow again. It was definitely the same bird, as it wasn't afraid of me. I ran inside, got some bread and started to feed it. The next day I saw it again and this time it let me feed it with my fingers. By the end of the week it was sitting on my hand. One of the most bizarre incidents with this sparrow was when I was sitting in my living room with my husband and the sparrow started to walk in through the sliding door.

About a week later my mother came round to visit me. I'd been so preoccupied with my husband's poor health that I had neglected her. She looked really well and happy, though, which surprised me, as I knew how much she had suffered since Dad's funeral. She told me that a sparrow had been following her and she had even bought a photograph of herself feeding it with her fingers. She told me that it had even flown by her earlier that day when she had been driving over to visit me.

My mum and I are totally convinced that this sparrow was delivering a message from Dad. Whenever I look at my favourite photo of Dad with a sparrow in his hand, it seems too coincidental for the sparrow not to be a messenger from the angels.

I've heard many stories like this about birds or other wild animals that are somehow able to ease the grief of those who have lost loved ones. I've also heard stories of animals communicating messages of hope and harmony at exactly the right moment. Here's Elaine's story:

Water Ballet

Last summer I went on the trip of a lifetime to the United States with my husband Simon. We were walking along the shores of a river when suddenly four dolphins appeared and started to 'dance' just for us, or so it seemed. A couple of pelicans overhead began to join in and it looked as though they were copying the dolphins' movement as they circled and spiralled and dived in and out of the water. Then two manatees started to join the water ballet. It was a stunning and unforgettable sight and so perfectly choreographed I half-expected a sea lion to appear with a baton to conduct them.

Such a sight would have been incredible at any time in our lives, but there could have been no better timing than this. We had gone on vacation with heavy hearts, having just lost a dear friend in a mugging that had turned violent. We had both felt numbed by the extensive media coverage and had increasingly begun to feel that we were living in a world where violence and terror were all-encompassing. When we saw our water ballet it was as if the creatures were saying, 'Don't give up. Look at us, we just keep on dancing through life's ups and downs.' Our hearts and our spirits were restored by that beautiful sight and we returned home determined to survive and thrive just like the lovely creatures who had danced to the rhythm of life for us.

Although I now believe there is a divine spark in all living beings, including animals, this wasn't always the case. When I was at school I was taught the Darwinian notion that life on Earth is all about the survival of the fittest. There seemed no place within the law of the jungle for love, generosity and compassion, but as the stories in this chapter have shown, animals can act with compassion and courage. Like us, they can experience and share love, and like us, they have souls – souls that, as this next section shows, are immortal.

Animals and the Afterlife

Love, whether it is in human or animal form, can cross the boundaries of space and time and many people who have lost beloved pets believe that their animals continue to visit them in spirit. After my cat Roddy died at the grand old age of 18 I would often sense her presence or feel the brush of her body against my legs. I was never frightened by these experiences – quite the contrary, they seemed the most comforting and natural thing in the world. And the more stories I hear from people who have had similar experiences, the more convinced I am that contact with a deceased family pet is possible.

As I was writing this chapter I got a great e-mail from a lady called Angel and given the appropriateness of her name and the great timing of her story, I knew I had to include it here.

Topaz

I hope you'll enjoy reading about my dog, Topaz. I got her when she was about three years old. I didn't know her exact age, as I got her from the dogs' home. We shared the next 15 years together and she was the most affectionate, loving and protective dog. During our years together whenever I was putting my make-up on, she would walk around me and lick my legs. Even if she was asleep, she would just know when I was getting ready to go out and after she had licked me she would sit next to me and watch me get ready.

Topaz died on the day before my fiftieth birthday. I was so upset I couldn't go in to work. Instead I went for a walk in the park where I had taken Topaz every day until her bladder infection got so serious she could barely move. I sat by the river and listened to the birds singing and the water flowing and was aware of the comforting presence of nature supporting me. In my heart I talked to Topaz and I thanked her for all the wonderful times we had had together. I thanked her for her love and her devotion and prayed to the angels to take care of her in heaven.

The next morning I got up and started to put on my make-up ready for work. Memories of Topaz flooded into my mind and I felt numb again with grief. I simply couldn't lift my lipstick or my foundation. And then I felt a little lick on my ankles in the same spot that Topaz had always licked me before. I wasn't imagining it – I could actually feel it. It was gentle and light, but there was no mistaking it. I looked down and I actually saw Topaz looking up at me the way she had done before she got ill. The vision lasted for several minutes. I realized that Topaz wanted me to know that she was still looking out for me and that it was time to get back into my life. She kept sitting there until my make-up was done and then with one last twirl around my legs she was gone.

I only ever saw Topaz that once after she died, but it was more than enough. She came back to teach me that when love is genuine and true, death can't put a stop to it because it lasts forever.

Mandy's story also proves that when animals die the smile they leave behind in our hearts never fades:

Bobby

Bobby was a black giant of a dog, a Great Dane who weighed in at an impressive 137 lb when he was four years old and fully grown. I got used to the 'Is that a horse?' or 'Who's walking who?' comments every time I took him for a walk in the streets or the park. Sometimes people fearful of his size would cross the road when they saw me walking towards them. How wrong they were to be afraid of a dog that had a heart of gold.

Bobby was my gentle giant. Living alone as a single woman I never felt afraid at night, as I knew he would take care of me. Once a burglar tried to break in, but he soon disappeared when Bobby bounded down the stairs.

As a special needs teacher I would often talk about Bobby to my pupils and they loved to see pictures of him. I'd take him into work every now and again, with the school's permission, and he loved being the centre of attention. He seemed to know why he was visiting the children and could always make them laugh. There was one little girl, Julie, who seemed to come alive when Bobby was on the scene. Her parents noticed and that Christmas she got the present of her dreams – a puppy.

One sad day in March 2007 I got a call from my mum, who walked Bobby during the day when I was at work, telling me that Bobby wasn't his usual bouncy self. The moment my working day was over I rushed home and as soon as I saw Bobby I knew that something wasn't right. I took him to the vet and my worst fear was confirmed. The vet told me that Bobby was bleeding internally from either a suspected bleeding disorder or rat poison and the only thing that could be done was to put him out of his misery.

As Bobby lay dying in my arms and I felt the life within him fade away, I tried to comfort him as best I could. To the last he didn't complain and gave me looks that comforted me. We had the deepest connection and as he passed I could sense that he knew how much I would miss him. It took three hours for him to die and during that time I remembered every time we had napped together, played together and laughed together. I had never experienced such love for a living creature as I did then.

My love and connection with Bobby did not end with his death. He visited me in my dreams for several weeks afterwards. In some of my dreams everything seemed so real – his tail wagging, his gentle strength and the sound of his breath – that when I woke up I half-expected him to be lying beside me.

Although the dreams were a source of comfort, there were times when I found the loss unbearable, but one night all that changed when I suddenly felt something jumping on my bed and giving my hand a love bite. It was Bobby. I couldn't see him, yet I was wide awake and knew that he had come in spirit to comfort me and say goodbye.

Now I celebrate the happy years I had with Bobby. It's a tremendous joy to show my pupils his pictures, to discover his hairs and whiskers still clinging to clothes or furniture and to smell his scent still lingering on toys. I try to preserve all these reminders even though I am aware that a time will come when they will fade away. But somehow this doesn't matter as much as it might once have done because I know in my heart that my gentle, loving giant will be travelling with me forever.

Mandy and Angel are just two of the many people all over the world who feel that the bond they have with their pets remains unbroken by death. The love pets can offer us in this life and the next is unquestioning, uncritical, unconditional and constant. They can calm us with their presence and offer us comfort and strength when we need it most. Angels come in all shapes and sizes and, as the stories in this chapter have shown, for people who feel connected to their pets, some even have four (or more!) legs.

Chapter 7

From Cradle to Beyond the Grave

Beside each man who's born on earth
A guardian angel takes his stand
To guide him through life's mysteries.

Meander of Athens

So far the majority of stories you've read have been about adults whose lives have been transformed by angels, but in this chapter you'll see that miraculous experiences can happen at any stage in a person's life from the very beginning to the grave and beyond.

Any woman who has been pregnant will know that it is one of the most traumatic yet amazing experiences, so it is hardly surprising that many angel stories are associated with the miracle of new life. Doreen had a visitation in the last moments of her pregnancy and here, in her own words, is her story:

'Won't Be Long Now'

My baby was due on 16 October 1990, but my doctor arranged an appointment for me to be induced a few weeks early as scans showed the baby was getting larger and larger and I'm quite a small woman. One week before I was due to go into hospital for my induction I wrote a long e-mail to my sister in Canada, telling her not to worry and that I would be fine. When I had finished and turned off my computer I looked up and saw a young man in a cream gown that was solid yet transparent, if that makes sense. He was standing in front of the bookcase in my study and he held a baby in his arms. He came closer to me and held the baby out for me to see. She looked about six months old and she had a bruise on her forehead that curved in a banana shape. The man smiled and although he didn't say anything I knew that he was telling me that it wouldn't be long now and my baby would arrive very soon. Then, still smiling, he glided away and vanished, with the baby still staring at me.

Nothing like this had ever happened to me before and at the time I put it down to tiredness and anxiety about the birth of my first baby. I didn't tell my husband about my experience as I knew he wouldn't have believed a word I said. That night I couldn't sleep and after a few hours tossing and turning, I suddenly felt dampness between my legs – my waters had broken. I woke my husband, who got me to hospital in record time, and 20 hours later baby Christine was born.

I didn't get to hold my baby right away as she was three weeks premature and the doctors wanted to make sure she was healthy, but after half an hour or so a midwife came in with her in her arms. She told me that she was a little weak after the birth but she would be just fine. Then before she handed her to me she told me not to be alarmed by the bruising on her forehead as it looked worse than it was. She told me that it had been caused by the instrument the doctor had used to grip her head to help her through the birth canal and that although there might be a scar it would not be an unsightly one.

As the midwife handed the bundle to me I stared into my baby's wise blue eyes. It didn't feel like the first time we had seen each other because we had met the evening before when the angel had visited me.

Seventeen years on Christine still has the remains of the scar on her forehead, but she's never been self-conscious about it because I've always told her that it's the mark her angel left behind to remind her how special she is.

Lara also 'met' her children before they were born:

'Can't Wait to Meet You'

I'd always wanted a really large family, at least five or six children, so it was heartbreaking when after the birth of my first two children I had a miscarriage followed by another miscarriage. Then I got pregnant and the scan showed twins. I didn't want to take any risks this time so for the first three months I was on bed rest.

One night I had a dream in which I met a woman with a white gown and purple wings. Holding her hands were two children, a boy with blond hair and a girl with brown hair. The woman was smiling, but there were also tears in her eyes when she said, 'Your children can't wait to meet you.' I woke up feeling elated, but my elation turned to despair the following morning when I started to cramp with familiar pains and I lost my twins. I had to deliver them naturally and it was the most painful and traumatic experience I have ever had to face.

After the miscarriage of my twins I started to think that perhaps my vision of a large family wasn't to be. My doctor was concerned that another pregnancy might be risky, so I made the painful decision to stop trying for another baby. Imagine my surprise ten months later when contraception failed and I found out I was pregnant again. I went for my scan and could not believe my eyes and ears when I was told once again that I was having twins. My doctor said that the odds of this happening were incredible.

The pregnancy was a tough one but I didn't lose my babies this time and eventually a beautiful boy and girl were born. They are three years old now and they look exactly like they did when I met them in my dream.

As well as stories about visitations before a baby is born I've been sent many stories about angelic experiences happening during childbirth. Sometimes the vision of an angel appears but on other occasions, as when my daughter was born, comfort and strength are offered by a gentle, reassuring voice from beyond. And after giving birth, many women have some amazing experiences, like this one sent to me by a lady called Annie:

Nurse Hope

It wasn't easy for me to get pregnant. We tried for years and eventually at the age of 42 I got my miracle. The pregnancy went well until the seventh month, when my blood pressure went sky high. I went into labour and my baby was born weighing 4 lb 9 oz. She looked so tiny as I was wheeled in to see her in the incubator, but the love I felt for her was instant.

Then a doctor gave me the bombshell I had not expected: my little girl had Down's syndrome. He told me that normally this kind of thing was detected during scans in the pregnancy but on rare occasions such as this such disorders were not picked up.

My husband held me for several minutes after he was also told the news. We were heartbroken, confused and depressed and I wept and wept and wept. A paediatrician came to see us, but he wasn't very reassuring. My doctor suggested antidepressants, which I refused. Then a different nurse came round to see us. She didn't say anything at first. She simply tidied my room and asked if I wanted a cup of tea. There was something very comforting about her, so I said, 'Yes,' and when she came back with my cup of tea she brought one for herself as well and sat down at the bottom of my bed. She told me she had a friend who had a child with Down's and the child had brought everyone so much happiness. She stayed for at least an hour and just talked to me about her friend's son and how Down's children were like any other children and all they really needed was their parents' love. She helped me calm down and get everything in perspective. She didn't tell me her name, but on her uniform I saw a name label and it read 'Nurse Hope'.

When my little girl hit 5 lb I was finally able to take her home. I'm not saying it was easy, as it wasn't, but thanks to Nurse Hope I knew that I could do it.

When we had settled into a routine at home I went back to the hospital to thank everyone and take some pictures to update them. I especially wanted to see Nurse Hope, but no one seemed to know who she was. I have no idea whether that kind woman was an angel or a nurse, but her visit 30 years ago gave me the courage and confidence I needed to take care of my beautiful child.

Whether she was an angel or not, one thing is certain – the aptly named Nurse Hope gave Annie the confidence and strength she needed at a traumatic moment in her life.

It's not just new mothers but also their babies who are reassured by angels. The sheer volume of stories I've received about babies and angels has led me to believe that perhaps we are all born with the ability to see and trust angels but as time passes and we get older it gets suppressed. Countless new parents have told me that their babies will often stare, chuckle or even lift their arms towards a spot in the room that is empty and they can think of no logical explanation for this. When my own children were babies I can recall many times when I was holding or feeding them and they would suddenly stop looking at me and look directly above my head or to the side of it. I'd try to get their attention back to me, but their eyes always travelled back to the spot that enchanted them. Sometimes they would open their little mouths wide in wonder and at other times they would chuckle as if someone was making funny faces or playing peek-a-boo. I used to think this was just their eyes and brain learning to focus, but now I know that it was an angel on my shoulder.

There will always be people who will try to offer a rational explanation for experiences like this, but in the following two stories, both involving babies, I'm sure you'll agree that angelic intervention is the only possible explanation.

This first story, from Kenya, got such a lot of media coverage back in 2005 that you may already be familiar with it:

One of Those Amazing Things

Witness Stephen Tova told the independent *Daily Nation* newspaper that he saw a dog carrying a baby wrapped in a black dirty cloth crossing the road. He was shocked at first but when he tried to get a closer look the dog ran through a fence and disappeared along a dirt road. The report continues:

The infant was discovered after two children alerted adults that they had heard the sound of a baby crying near their wooden and corrugated-iron shack. Residents found the baby lying next to the dog and her own pup. The dog reportedly dragged the baby across a busy road and through some barbed wire to a shed in the poor Nairobi neighbourhood where puppies from two stray dogs were sheltering.

When the story broke well-wishers from Kenya and all over the world sent messages to the country's main hospital to enquire about adopting the child, who was aptly named Angel. The stray dog that saved the child was also taken into care, although her last surviving puppy died for unknown reasons. Animal welfare officials named the dog Mkombozi, or Saviour.

The dog, a tan short-haired mixed breed who was heavy with milk from nursing, was possibly trying to care for the child because most of her puppies had died, but the case was very unusual, as other stray dogs would have just left her to die, so why didn't this one?

Many people at the time talked about guardian angels, but the implications of this miracle reached far wider than the child involved because it drew much-needed attention to the widespread problem of abandoned babies in Kenya, where poverty and failed relationships are frequently to blame.

At first there was a great deal of scepticism about this story, but government spokesman Alfred Mutua investigated it and later stated that the report was correct. In his opinion it was one of those amazing things that defy human explanation and indicate that somebody is out there watching over us.

This second story didn't hit the headlines in quite the same way, but when it happened to astonished mother Sarah it felt every bit as remarkable:

Falling Down

Sammy was three months old when an angel saved her life. I was having a picnic in the park with my sister and her little girl, Laura, who was four at the time and pushing her own dolls' pram. It was a beautiful day with clear blue skies and a light breeze. After pushing Sammy around in her pram for a while, we decided to find a nice shady place under a tree to sit down and tuck into our picnic. While my sister got everything ready I fed Sammy until she got sleepy and then settled her down in her pram for a nap with the brakes on. Determined to make the most of whatever free time I had while my baby slept, I enjoyed a sandwich and an ice-cold drink and then moved out of the shade to lie down and soak up some sun with my sister.

It's a bit of a blur what happened next, but it felt as though someone had punched me in the stomach. I opened my eyes and it wasn't a person but the branch of a tree that had fallen onto me. I couldn't believe it, but a huge branch from the tree we had been sitting under had crashed down. My sister and I had avoided the worst of it because we had edged out towards the sunshine, but my heart stood still when I saw the wheels of Sammy's pram spinning away and the pram crushed underneath the heavy branch.

By now quite a few people were gathering round. A man helped me lift the branch from the pram. I felt sick with worry. Sammy wasn't in there.

Then I heard shouting. It was my sister yelling. She was telling me that Laura was holding my baby. Although we had told her time and time again not to disturb Sammy or try to pick her up, as she might drop her, I could not have been happier with her for disobeying me this time. Laura loved newborns and as soon as she had seen my sister and I asleep in the sun she had discarded her baby doll and seized her chance to play at being a real mummy.

If Laura hadn't taken Sammy out of the pram she would almost certainly have been seriously injured or even died, so on that day she was her angel. We often expect our children to do as they are told and get frustrated when they don't, but, as Sarah's story shows, sometimes it may be better to let children follow their instincts and, as Trudie's story shows, their psychic potential. Trudie explains:

Typical Toddler?

In nearly every respect my son Jonathon, aged three, is a typical toddler. He has tantrums for sure, but although he can be the most difficult and stubborn child at times he can also be the most delightful. He seems to be able to read my mind and sometimes just looking at him can lift my spirits after a tough day. He also has the most incredible imagination. One day he is a soldier on a mission, the next he is Spider Man and the next he is on a mission to Mars. He also has a really special bond with my father. They have a secret language and a shared sense of humour. When Jonathon can't get to sleep my dad entertains him or tells him stories and if he wakes up after a night terror my dad is the first to come and soothe him. The most extraordinary thing about all this is that my father died four years ago.

I have no idea how Jonathon knows so much about a grandfather he never met. Sometimes I'll stand outside the door of his room when he is playing or talking to my dad and will hear him mention things, people and places he has never seen, met or been to. I will sit and listen to him tell me about his granddad's stamp collection or relatives I didn't even know I had.

When all this started about a year ago I didn't worry because everybody told me Jon was just going through the imaginary friend stage. My mum told me that I needed to make sure he got more fresh air and exercise. My husband told me to cut down on the Disney videos. Nothing made any difference and it's clear to me now that this is so much more than an imaginary friend. Jonathon is actually communicating with Dad. I know this because Dad came to visit me once too.

My husband was out late one night and I was on my own reading in bed when I felt a slight movement as if someone had gently patted my leg. I looked down and saw an indentation at the bottom of the bed, like the shape of a fist, and it seemed to be moving. Then the curtains started to move too and I was overtaken by a most wonderful feeling. My heart beat loudly and my body tingled and I felt surrounded by warmth and love. I closed my eyes to drink in the sensation and even though I felt a little scared I said out loud, 'Dad, I know you are here. I'm not scared and thank you for taking care of Jonathon for me.'

Then I heard the door shut downstairs and the familiar sound of my husband putting his keys in the bowl in the hall. Suddenly the energy rushed out of me and I was left feeling light and peaceful.

My father has never visited me again but I know he continues to visit Jonathon. Some nights I will go into Jonathon's room and find him snoring loudly in his bed. I'll look around and see toys scattered on the floor, toys that I know were packed away on high shelves when I put

Jonathon to bed. Nobody in my family believes in life after death, but I'm going to be the first to break with tradition. I believe that my dad spends more time with Jonathon than anyone else he knows. Every night now when I kiss Jonathon good night and turn out the lights I smile to myself and wish my dad a silent good night too.

Crystal Children

Many people describe babies as angels. Their cute smiles and knowing looks are doted upon, but all too often when the babies become toddlers their spontaneous and instinctive approach to life isn't encouraged in the same way. If a child does have a psychic experience it can become very confusing for a parent, especially if that parent does not believe in angels themselves. Some parents may wonder if there is something wrong with their child, but let me assure you that if a child talks about angels there is absolutely nothing wrong with them. Angelic intervention is just as common – if not more common – in the lives of children as it is in adults, because children have the receptivity and trust that adults often lack. As adults, our task should be to support and nurture the spiritual openness of childhood, not to suppress it.

You may have heard of a select group of children sent from heaven to save us all from ourselves and raise the spiritual consciousness of the world. These children are called 'indigo' or 'rainbow children' in reference to the aura of colours or the energy field surrounding them. Another term used to describe them is 'crystal children', because they seem to have special psychic abilities. There is a whole industry of books and websites devoted to these children, with profiles and personality checklists, but in short a maturity beyond their years, an extraordinary awareness and what seems like psychic ability are typical characteristics.

The idea of children saving the world has obvious appeal, but I am apprehensive whenever I hear talk of a 'super race' or select group of children who are a part of the natural evolution of humankind. What about all the other children who don't demonstrate these powers or personality traits? Anyone whose life has been touched by an angel will know that to angels every single child is special, and every child, whether they demonstrate psychic potential or not, is a miracle sent from heaven to save us from ourselves.

Here are two stories that really caught my eye because, until their otherworldly encounters, neither of the children involved had ever demonstrated any psychic potential or interest in angels. Let's start with Jenny's story:

'What Was your Day Like?'

Life gets so busy sometimes that we forget to focus on what really matters. Ever since my husband left me for another woman when my boys were both under five years old I have had to do everything myself. Fortunately my income has always been enough to make sure my boys have food, clothes and a roof over their head, but we have never had anything left over for luxuries.

For the first five years I guess I just went into survival mode – wake up, get the kids to nursery or school, go to work, collect the kids, cook, shop, clean, put the kids to bed, catch up on more work and then fall asleep. Week-days were a feat of organization, especially when the boys started going to after-school clubs and their friends' houses. Every other weekend my ex would pick them up, but I'd spend most of that 'free' time tidying, cooking and preparing for the week ahead.

When Felix, my elder son, was nine, I was up for promotion at work and working extra hard to prove that I was up to the job. On the day of my interview he had a school trip to a nature park and I can vaguely remember him asking me the night before for some spending money to take with him. I was so stressed about the promotion, though, that I completely forgot to give him the funds he needed. The interview went well and later that evening I got a call telling me that I had got the job. It was a huge relief. I poured myself a large glass of wine and went to join the boys to watch TV.

I gave Felix a cuddle as I sat down and suddenly remembered that I hadn't asked him about his school trip. He said it had been great and that he had really enjoyed it, although he had hated sitting on the back seat of the coach because it had made him feel sick. I asked him what he had seen in the park and he answered, 'I saw deer and animals and stuff and I also saw Nana standing next to the stump of a really old oak tree. That stump was amazing. It had hundreds and hundreds of rings.'

I tried to stay calm because my mum was in a nursing home in the advanced stages of Alzheimer's and my ex's mum was abroad. I asked Felix if he meant his grandma on his father's side, but he shook his head and insisted that he had seen Nana. He was a level-headed boy who never lied or made things up, so I asked him if Nana had said anything to him and he replied, 'No, she just gave me a big bear hug and then a couple of pounds to spend in the gift shop 'cause you forgot to give it to me in the morning. I could see her, Mummy, but when she hugged me I didn't feel it.'

After I had put Felix and his brother to bed that night I couldn't get Mum out of my mind. I decided to visit the nursing home in the morning, but I never got to see my mother again. At a few minutes past midnight I got a call saying that she had passed away peacefully in her sleep.

I asked why I hadn't been warned and they told me that they were as surprised by her sudden death as I was.

Even though I miss Mum, I feel so grateful that the one person I feared my children would never know is still a part of our lives.

Felix's matter-of-fact attitude towards angels is fairly typical of children and if his mum had not asked him how his day had been he might never have mentioned his experience to her. Here's another story, sent in by Paula, about a child's common-sense approach to the other world:

Right in Front of your Eyes

In March 2007 my mother passed away unexpectedly from a stroke after a routine operation. She was only in her early sixties, so my grief was very intense.

A few weeks after her death I went to stay for a few days with my best friend Jo and her husband Rob. I'd known Jo ever since we'd been next-door neighbours as children. She and Rob had a two-and-a-half-year-old daughter called Ruby.

Jo and I were talking about Mum one morning and Ruby was in the room with us, playing with her dolls. She had met my mum on a couple of occasions and had always had a lot of fun with her. Mum loved kids and would play with Ruby so that I could have the chance to put my feet up and chat to my friend.

After Jo and I had chatted for a while Ruby called out for my mum as she always used to. Jo gently reminded her that she was in heaven so she couldn't play now. Ruby looked at her and said, 'No, no, Mama, she is sitting right there,' and she pointed to a spot on the floor next to her dolls. Jo asked her, 'Where is she?' and Ruby pointed to the same spot and replied, 'Right here, playing with me.' She was absolutely convinced that my mum was in the room with us and, you know what, I believe her.

Children have such a refreshing, enthusiastic, unquestioning attitude towards angels that they can often see far more of them than adults. Traditionally, there has always been a close association between angels and children, but sadly, as we get older, peer pressure, scepticism and fear of ridicule often repress this innocent spirituality. I sincerely hope that reading this book will help you to reconnect with your inner child so you can once again look at the world with excitement and enthusiasm and see angels through the eyes of child.

Angels Are Always with Us

Stories about children and angels tend to generate a lot of interest, but over the years I have also noticed an increasing number of stories about the close bond that exists between angels and teenagers. Leaving childhood behind can be a daunting experience these days, with exams, hormones, family dynamics and romance to contend with, and that's not forgetting the looming backdrop of war, politics and climate change. With organized religion no longer providing the structure and certainty that it used to, it is no surprise to me that more and more teenagers are anxious to believe that there is something more than material world and that they have their very own guardian angel by their side.

An interesting feature of stories sent to me by teens is that however unlikely the places or ways the angels choose to reveal themselves, angelic encounters always provide the comfort and reassurance that many teenagers so desperately need in this tough world. Here is a special example, sent to me by 15-year-old Cassie:

Must Be an Angel

I was incredibly close to my big sister Carrie. She was more than my sister, she was my best friend. Sure, we had our quarrels, but we always made up and life was sweet again. She died when I was a few days away from my thirteenth birthday. She was just 17. One morning she was there, laughing as she put on her makeup, and the next she was gone. A car hit her as she crossed the road and she died a month later.

The thirteenth year of my life was dreadful. At first I couldn't accept that my sister was gone and then, when reality set in, I got very depressed. I didn't leave my room for a whole two days on one occasion. I knew that my parents were incredibly worried and that my behaviour was making their grief so much harder to bear, but I didn't care. Nothing seemed to matter anymore.

Sitting alone in my room one day, I heard a noise coming from Carrie's room. I went inside and everything was just as she had left it. My mum had always refused to change anything. There was something unusual, though – Carrie's laptop was lying on her bed and music was playing. The sound was muffled, so I listened with the earphones and heard 'There Must Be an Angel' by Annie Lennox. After the song the laptop switched itself off.

Mum and Dad are sceptical, but I've tried to think of a rational explanation for what happened and there is no way Carrie's laptop could have switched itself on like that, as I was alone in the house at the time. And even if it had, why, out of the thousands of songs Carrie had on it, did that particular song have to play? Music meant a lot to

Carrie and I think she chose it as a medium to say good-bye to me. It never happened again, but the comfort I got from the experience was incredibly reassuring. Knowing my sister is not far away has made it so much easier to get back into my life.

Adults of every age can learn a lot from the way young people like Carrie are able to draw inspiration and comfort from angelic experiences without fear or mistrust. I truly believe that the way forward for the human race is to stop doubting and suppressing the enthusiasm and openness of children and to nurture and celebrate their innocent spirituality instead. And the best way to do this is to listen more, judge less and set a positive and inspiring example of love, trust, and open-mindedness ourselves.

As the extraordinary true stories in this book have tried to explain, angels walk by our side from our birth through our childhood, teenage and adult years to our old age. It is a blessing to know that they are always with each and every one of us, offering comfort and hope. And it is a blessing also to know that they will be with us when our lives end. Here is Vicky's story:

Illumination

A day before my 98-year-old mother fell into a sleep she would never wake up from she told me that her bedroom was filled with glowing beings of light. They were all singing and they lifted her up and took her to a place where she could run as she had when she was a little girl. She said she felt weightless and the place had green meadows and flowers and although everything was illuminated, there was no sunlight. Then the glowing beings brought her back to her bed and kissed her cheek, leaving her with whispered promises to return soon.

My mum said she thought the glowing beings were angels because they were so tender and loving and had wings that shimmered like diamonds. She told me that she wasn't afraid to die anymore because she knew she was going to somewhere beautiful and full of light.

I sat up with Mum on the night she stopped breathing. I was dozing by her side and woke with a start when a book I'd been reading fell to the floor. I heard my mum moan softly and then I saw what looked like a silver cloud drift up towards the ceiling. A hand reached down and pulled the cloud until it disappeared. I'm convinced that this was the hand of one of the glowing beings Mum had spoken about the day before.

Many people have told me similar stories about loved ones being comforted by the presence of angels or lost loved ones in spirit close to or at the moment of death. Medication and hallucination are two well-known explanations for deathbed visions, but whatever you choose to believe there is no doubt that in the overwhelming majority of cases these visions not only bring comfort and reassurance to those who are close to death but also to those they leave behind.

Near-Death Experiences

Equally amazing are the stories of people who have visited the afterlife but not died. Typically these near-death experiences, or NDEs, happen when a person's life hangs by a thread or when their heart has temporarily stopped. The experience is far more common than you might think and I just wish I had the space in this book to share some of the hundreds of incredible NDE stories that have come to me. Perhaps that's another book! For now I just want to say that in the overwhelming majority of cases people who have had near-death experiences are left with a lingering sense of wonder and enchantment. In Elizabeth's case, the experience of leaving her physical body behind was so intoxicating that she has lost all fear of death:

'The Day I Died'

In 1991 I died in a car crash. I remember chatting with my friend in the back seat one moment and seeing the fear in her eyes the next as a car crashed into the side of us. The next thing I can remember is travelling at lightning speed and being dazzled by a golden light. It felt like one of those fun rides you go on at a theme park – not the ones that make you want to throw up, the ones that make you giggle.

It took a while for my eyes to adjust and the travelling sensation to stop and then I found myself in a golden room. In this room I remembered everything about my life and felt every emotion I have ever felt. I also felt the impact that my life had had on others, both the good and the bad. I felt the pain I had caused my mum when I ran away from home, the anger I had caused my sister when I had stolen her shoes and clothes. I felt everything. After I had remembered my life, my next instinct was to laugh. I laughed because I felt light, free and happy. I was also laughing at myself and all the times in my life that I had got worked up about things that didn't really matter.

Then someone came to meet me. It was my aunt. She'd always been a bit of a rebel and as I was growing up she'd been the only person I really felt understood me. I missed her wisdom terribly when she died.

She took me by the hand and we both laughed and danced with happiness. The feeling of elation was so incredible.

Suddenly I was looking down at two cars mangled together. Traffic was backed up on both sides of the road and there was a great deal of confusion. I saw two men rush towards the scene with green outfits and white cases. I watched as they lifted my head and shone lights into my eyes. My friend in the car was standing on the side of the road sobbing and her mum, who was also sobbing, was being carried away on a stretcher.

That was when I remembered my accident and as I did so I started to melt back into my body. I remember wanting to make a difference with my life and focus more on my life purpose. I also remember not wanting to leave my aunt but feeling reassured that I would see her again soon, as spiritual time is measured very differently from physical time.

I was halfway back into my body when I stopped and tried to pull back towards my aunt, who was still hovering by my side. Then I looked over at my sobbing friend. As soon as the thought of my death and how the trauma of it would impact her life formed in my mind, I was back in my body. I opened my eyes and instantly recognized the two paramedics bending over me. Later, in the ambulance, I told them about my experience on the other side, which I now know is called a near-death experience. They didn't seem surprised at all. I guess they probably hear about it all the time in their job.

My experience has taught me that everything we do in this life is remembered in the next and that if we knowingly cause others pain and upset we will relive that when we pass on. It also taught me that my life has a purpose and that I should not worry so much about things that really don't matter. Twenty-five years later there isn't a day that goes by that I don't draw strength, hope and inspiration from my experience because I know that death isn't an ending but a wonderful new beginning where there is love and laughter. Do I fear death? Not in the slightest. On the day I 'died' I never felt so alive.

It is a blessing to know that angels are with us not only to our last breath but in the world beyond our last breath. In both this life and the next they are watching over and waiting for us.

Yours Sincerely

And so as this chapter and indeed this book draws to a close we come full circle with a tender story sent to me eight years ago by a gentleman who didn't leave his name. He simply ended his letter with the words 'yours sincerely'. I'm closing with his story because as heart-wrenching as it is, it shows us that angels truly are with us from cradle to beyond the grave.

> My grandson died last spring. He was a sick baby from the start and he only lived for eight short weeks. Nothing would have made me happier than to see my third grandchild grow up, but it wasn't meant to be.
>
> My son and his wife were in great distress and I'd have given anything to ease their pain, but the manner of my grandson's death brought some comfort and healing. We had been told by the hospital that he didn't have long and as we gathered around his cot he opened his eyes for the first time since he was born. He looked at his mother and father first for several seconds and then he looked at me. It was a look of understanding and connection I will never ever forget. Then he moved his little head and looked at the ceiling. As he did so, he raised his arms and started to smile. That smile stayed on his face as he closed his eyes and gently died.
>
> I know there may be medical explanations for his fleeting moment of lucidity at the point of death but they don't interest me. What mattered to us all that day was that we believed there was an angel in the room waiting to carry him to heaven and comforting him with a smile …

Think of this book as an arrow to heaven, a reminder of the constant loving presence of angels in your life from cradle to beyond the grave. Use it for strength, guidance and encouragement whenever you feel the need of an angel. As well as being wonderful, life can sometimes be painful and it can be very heartening to know that however difficult it gets your very own guardian angel is standing close by your shoulder, watching and waiting for you to accept that angels are in your heart and on your side.

So accept that angels are always beside you and within you. Accept that they want you to smile. Trust that they want you to love. Believe that they want you to fly.

Afterword: Look Up

The golden moments in the stream of life rush
past us and we see nothing but sand; the
angels come to visit us, and we only know
them when they are gone.

George Eliot

I'd like to think that the stories in this book have shown
you what an important part angels can play in your life if
you are willing to open your mind and your heart and
believe that they are always close by. Angels protect us
and are ready to assist in the lightening of our earthly
burdens, if we ask. As soon as we tune in to their
wonderful energy we are aware of the love that
surrounds us. Their presence leaves a bright spark in our
heart which can never be forgotten.

This doesn't necessarily mean, however, that if you
believe in angels your life will be easy and that you won't
have any more problems to deal with. Although the

purpose of angels is to guide us through times of difficulty and danger and help us fulfil our dreams, there are certain things we need to experience that are beyond their control.

Why bad things happen to good people is a spiritual question that we will never be able to answer in our human form. What we do know is that the harder the experience, the more we learn and the more our souls grow, so it is possible that tough experiences, like divorce, redundancy or, worse still, the loss of a loved one, are all difficulties we can gather incredible strength from. This can sometimes make life seem very unjust and painful, but angels can remind us that it is how we handle situations and move on from distressing circumstances that strengthens our character and gives our soul wings.

So, even if angels can't take away the hard lessons that you need to learn during your lifetime, never forget that testing times can often bring positive changes. If I hadn't felt really low in the first year of my daughter's life I would never have ended up writing about angels. And I've lost count of the times that people have told me that, although they would not have believed it at the time, the hardship, trauma or grief they have endured in the past has strengthened them emotionally or spiritually or changed the direction of their life in a positive way. Every time someone finds an inner strength they didn't

know they had or regains hope in the face of disillusion-
ment, every time something good comes out of something bad, angels can be seen at work.

It's a universal truth that the more we trust and
believe in angels, the more they will grace our lives with
their loving presence, but it is important to remember
that angels can be found both outside and within us.
One of my favourite angelic blessings is: 'Wherever you
go, may your guardian angel be above you, below you,
beside you, in front of you, behind you and within you.'
It's special to me because it reminds me that we humans
are the intermediaries of angels on Earth and it is
through us that they can channel their energy and love.
In other words, we don't always need to search for angels
in the outside world, as the magic of our inner angel is
already within us, waiting for us to believe and trust in it.

Remember, your angels won't be able to work magic
in your life if you don't meet them halfway and ask for
help. You can do this by taking the time to sit still or
meditate quietly so that you can tune in to your intuition or hear the voice of your guardian angel. You can
do this by concentrating on your dreams and the special
messages they send. You can do this by paying attention
to the coincidences that surround you every day of your
life. You can do this by noticing angel calling cards or
signs or by letting animals and the natural world speak to
you. You can do this by simply looking up to the clouds

and thanking heaven for the angels and for all that is loving and good in this life.

I shall leave you for now with this beautiful quote from an unknown author:

'You don't have to study to become an angel –
just trust your heart and wing it!'